THE REED FIELD GUIDE TO

NEW ZEALAND
BIRDS

THE REED FIELD GUIDE TO
NEW ZEALAND
BIRDS

Geoff Moon

REED

Front cover: (clockwise) White Heron, Morepork
              chicks, Goldfinch, Takahe, Stitchbird.

Back cover: Pied Shag (top)
              Kaka (bottom)

Title page: Morepork chicks

Published by Reed Books, a division of Reed
Publishing (NZ) Ltd, 39 Rawene Road, Birkenhead,
Auckland. Associated companies, branches and
representatives throughout the world.

ISBN 0 7900 0504 2

Text and photographs copyright © Geoff Moon 1992

First published 1992
Reprinted 1994 (twice), 1996 (twice), 1998
Reprinted 2000

Printed in Singapore

Contents

Introduction

Within its small land mass, New Zealand has many different types of habitats where birds live, feed and breed. These localities of mountains, forests, wetlands, open country and coasts are all within easy reach of birdwatchers. This book illustrates with photographs all the species of birds which are likely to be seen in these habitats in the North, South and Stewart Islands and adjacent offshore islands.

Birds of the Chatham Islands and subantarctic islands have not been included. Neither have some of the very rare stragglers and vagrants which sometimes stray to our shores. Readers seeking information on these birds are recommended to refer to *Collins Guide to the Birds of New Zealand*, by R.A. Falla, R.B. Sibson and E.G. Turbott (Collins 1986), which gives full data and ornithological details of these species.

In some bird species sexual dimorphism occurs, where there is a marked difference in the plumage colour between the sexes. In each instance where this is evident, photographs have been included to illustrate this feature.

Taxonomists group birds into specific sections according to their anatomy. Closely related species are listed as a genus, while related genera are grouped together as a family. These families in turn are grouped to form an order. The first part of a bird's scientific name is the genus. The second name refers to the species, and the third name, where applicable. refers to the subspecies. Thus, dealing with the Kaka, the genus is *Nestor*, and the species is *meridionalis*. As there are subspecies for the North and the South Island Kaka, the subspecies name for the North Island Kaka is *septentrionalis* and for the South Island Kaka *meridionalis*. The closely related Kea is grouped in the same genus, *Nestor*, with its species name of *notabilis*. As there are no subspecies of the Kea, there is no third scientific name.

In this guide book, birds are dealt with in taxonomic order following that listed in the *Checklist of the Birds of New Zealand*, 3rd edition, compiled by the Checklist Committee (E.G. Turbott, Convener) of the Ornithological Society of New Zealand Inc., and published in 1990 by Random Century. According to the bird's anatomy, this starts with the Kiwi and ends with the Rook, one of the passerine birds. The size of each bird is given in centimetres, and is its length from bill tip to the tip of its tail and, in a few instances, the length of the legs extending beyond the tail. These measurements have been taken from those given in *Collins Guide to the Birds of New Zealand* referred to earlier.

In conclusion, I wish to record my appreciation to many friends who have helped me with advice, or have provided opportunities to obtain photographs. Special thanks in this respect to Peter Daniel, Don Hadden, Dick Hooper, John Kendrick, Don Merton, Murray Quinn, Dick Sibson, David Stonex, Dick Veitch and Rob Wheeldon. I would also like to thank Ray Richards for his advice and encouragement and Barbara Nielsen for her co-operation with the design of this book.

Geoff Moon

Birdwatching Equipment

With good eyesight it is possible to correctly identify many birds without using additional aids. However, some birds are too small or too difficult to approach, so optical aids are an advantage.

A wide range of binoculars and telescopes is available today, some costing less than $100, with higher quality instruments up to nearly ten times this price. Although many of the cheaper binoculars and telescopes give reasonably good central vision, they do not compare with the better brands for overall performance. Often, the focusing mechanism of the cheaper instruments shows signs of wear after a short period of use.

For general birdwatching, binoculars with a magnification of 7 or 8 times are ideal. Those with a magnification of 10 or 12 times are ideal for spotting birds at a distance, but they are much more difficult to hold steady in windy conditions and are heavy and more bulky to carry around. Roof prism binoculars, while a little more expensive than standard binoculars, are extremely lightweight and compact and easily fit in one's pocket.

For long-distance observation, particularly to identify small wading birds on beaches, small spotting telescopes are essential. It is necessary to mount these on a sturdy tripod as their interchangeable eyepieces allow magnifications of 25 times and more and cannot be hand-held without some support. Telescopes have their limitations and are difficult to use on actively moving birds.

Birdwatchers should always carry a notebook to record details of birds seen in certain locations, or to note any interesting patterns of behaviour.

Hides are commonly used by bird photographers to make a close approach to birds. These can be used to advantage when sited in an area where birds congregate. A good position is near a pool in hot weather to watch various species coming to drink or bathe. Another excellent position is on a shellbank or sandspit. The hide is occupied at mid tide, and when the birds are driven off their mudflat feeding grounds by the rising tide they will often congregate in large flocks close to the hide.

Hides positioned near nesting sites must be used with extreme caution. Birds can very easily be disturbed and may desert their nests when hides are used without very careful preparation. Before using hides at nesting sites it is essential to refer to some of the available books on bird photography for suitable methods. Lack of space here does not allow discussion on this subject.

Glossary

Aquatic: frequenting water.

Arboreal: frequenting trees.

Axillaries: the feathers of the 'armpit', where the wing joins the body of a bird.

Colonial: nesting in groups or colonies.

Cosmopolitan: frequenting many countries.

Coverts: small feathers which overlie the bases of the large wing and tail feathers, or which cover a structure (e.g. ear coverts).

Covey: a small flock of birds which feed and roost together (applies to game birds only).

Crepuscular: active at dusk and dawn.

Cryptic: a colouring which serves to conceal; camouflage.

Decurved: curved downward.

Dimorphic: having two colour forms. Sexual dimorphism implies a difference in shape, size or colour between the sexes, e.g. Paradise Duck (colour), New Zealand Falcon (size).

Diurnal: active during the day.

Eclipse plumage: dull-coloured plumage acquired after breeding.

Endemic: restricted to a certain area.

Feral: escaped from captivity or domesticity and now wild.

Flight feathers: the long, well developed feathers of the wing. (Divided into primary and secondary.)

Gape: the wide open mouth of nestling birds.

Immature: a young bird in a plumage stage between juvenile and adult.

Invertebrate: animal without a spinal column, e.g. insect, worm.

Juvenile: a young bird in its first feathered plumage.

Lamellae: sieve-like appendages to edge of bird's bill, used to filter organisms from the water, e.g. Shoveler Duck.

Lek: a place of courtship where males (especially Kakapo and some game birds) gather to perform displays to attract females. Females visit leks to mate but nest in isolation elsewhere.

Melanism: dark plumage phase, resulting from presence of melanin pigment in plumage.

Migrant: a bird that regularly moves to another area away from its breeding range.

Mollusc: an invertebrate having a soft body and often a hard outer shell, e.g. snails.

Mustelid: a member of polecat genus, e.g. stoats, ferrets, introduced to New Zealand and now wild.

Nocturnal: active at night.

Omnivorous: eating a variety of plant and animal food.

Pelagic: frequenting the open ocean.

Polygamous: mating with more than one member of the opposite sex.

Race: a population of a species occurring in a different geographic region, e.g. eastern race of Falcon.

Raptor: a bird of prey.

Scrape: a shallow depression in the ground made by a bird to serve as a nest.

Speculum: a distinctive coloured area on the wing, e.g. the brightly coloured patch on the secondary wing feathers of ducks.

Subspecies: a geographical population of a species which has some slight differences from others of a species.

Taxonomy: the science of classifying organisms according to their natural relationships.

Vagrant: a species which occurs in a given area very infrequently, and whose normal range is in another area.

Wattles: coloured fleshy tissue on either side of the gape of birds such as Kokako and Saddleback.

Order APTERYGIFORMES: Kiwis
Family APTERYGIDAE: Kiwis
Genus *Apteryx*

North Island Brown Kiwi *Apteryx australis mantelli* (Kiwi). 50 cm.
South Island Brown Kiwi *Apteryx australis australis* (Tokoeka).
Stewart Island Brown Kiwi *Apteryx australis lawryi* (Tokoeka).

Habitat and distribution: North Island Kiwi widely distributed in forested areas. High density in Northland native and exotic forests and scrubland. South Island Brown Kiwi confined to Fiordland and South Westland.

Characteristics: Flightless, nocturnal. Females are larger and have longer bills. Stewart Island subspecies is the largest of the Brown Kiwis and often forages in daytime.

Voice: Male utters repeated prolonged whistling calls. Female call is shorter and hoarser. Snuffling sounds when feeding.

Food: Insects, grubs, spiders, fallen fruits. Probes deeply in soft soil for earthworms leaving characteristic bore marks.

Breeding: Nest is burrow or depression under tree roots or hollow log. Clutch 1 or 2 very large off-white eggs laid at intervals of 10–30 days. Incubation by male, but Stewart Island female reported to share incubation. Incubation period 72–80 days, sometimes up to 90 days. Chicks first leave burrow when 4–9 days old.

North Island Brown Kiwi.

North Island Brown Kiwi feeding.
Four-day-old Brown Kiwi chick leaving nest burrow.

Genus *Apteryx*

Little Spotted Kiwi *Apteryx owenii* (Kiwi-pukupuku). 40 cm.
Great Spotted Kiwi *Apteryx haastii.* (Roa). 50 cm.

Habitat and distribution: Little Spotted Kiwi common on Kapiti Island after introductions in 1912. Recently introduced to Hen and Red Mercury Islands. Great Spotted Kiwi widespread in forests of Northwest Nelson and Paparoa Range. Few sightings in beech forests further south.

Characteristics: Little Spotted Kiwi recognised by small size and overall grey colour, with mottled and banded dark markings. Great Spotted Kiwi has similar colouring, with overall chestnut tinge to feathers of back. Large size. Females larger than males.

Voice: Little Spotted Kiwi male utters repeated shrill trilling whistle. Great Spotted Kiwi gives high-pitched vibrating whistle.

Food: Similar to that of Brown Kiwi.

Breeding: Little Spotted Kiwi nests in burrows and beneath tree roots. Incubation period 70–75 days by male. Great Spotted Kiwi incubation 75–85 days in captivity (not known in wild). Both species breed in captivity.

Great Spotted Kiwi.

Great Spotted Kiwi running.
Little Spotted Kiwi.

Order PODICIPEDIFORMES: Grebes
Family PODICIPEDIAE: Grebes
Genus *Podiceps*

Australasian Crested Grebe *Podiceps cristatus australis* (Puteketeke).
50 cm.

Habitat and distribution: Confined mainly to subalpine lakes east of Southern Alps. Also lowland lakes of Westland and Fiordland. Absent from North Island.

Characteristics: Sits low in water. Entirely aquatic; does not come on land. Dives when feeding, remaining submerged for 20 to 50 seconds.

Voice: Usually silent. In breeding seasons gives groans and occasional honks and growls.

Food: Dives for small fish and aquatic insects.

Breeding: Nests from November to January. Nest of reeds, water weeds and sticks is built on submerged willow branches or compacted reed beds. Clutch 2–5 white eggs which become stained. Both sexes incubate for 24–28 days. Chicks swim soon after hatching and are often carried on parents' backs. Fed on small fish and occasional small feathers.

Australasian Crested Grebe on nest.

Australasian Crested Grebe, male and female.
Australasian Crested Grebes, courtship display.

Genus *Poliocephalus*

New Zealand Dabchick *Poliocephalus rufopectus* (Weweia). 28 cm.

Habitat and distribution: North Island lakes, ponds and dams. Commonest on sand-dune lakes and lakes of central Volcanic Plateau. Post-nuptial flocks on lakes of Wairarapa and Manawatu. Now absent from South Island.

Characteristics: Entirely aquatic. Recognised by blunt rear and sharp bill. Dives for food, submerging for 10 to 25 seconds. Low, skimming flight during courtship. Thought to migrate to other lakes at night.

Voice: Usually silent, but weak chattering call and moan near nest.

Food: Dives for small fish, crustaceans, insects and tadpoles.

Breeding: Long nesting season, usually July to March. Floating nest of water weeds anchored to raupo or rushes. Also builds nests of weeds on firm ground under rock overhangs or boatsheds. Clutch of 2 or 3 white eggs which soon become stained after being covered with weed when bird leaves nest. Both sexes incubate for 21–24 days. Chicks carried on parents' backs.

Opposite: New Zealand Dabchick on nest.
New Zealand Dabchick.

18

New Zealand Dabchick with chicks.
New Zealand Dabchick with 2½-week-old chicks.

Genus *Tachybaptus*

Australian Little Grebe *Tachybaptus novaehollandiae novaehollandiae*. 25 cm.

Habitat and distribution: Self-introduced to New Zealand in recent years. A few birds widely scattered on small lakes in North and South Islands.

Characteristics: More wary than New Zealand Dabchick. Tends to hide in rushes when approached. Conspicuous yellow 'teardrop' below eye at base of bill.

Voice: A prolonged trill, but usually silent.

Food: Dives for small fish, tadpoles, crustaceans and insects.

Breeding: Floating nest of water weeds and rushes anchored to rushes or submerged willow branches. Clutch of 2–4 white eggs, which soon become stained, is laid September to January. Both parents incubate for 21–25 days.

Australian Little Grebe.

Order PROCELLARIIFORMES: Tube-nosed birds
Family DIOMEDEIDAE: Albatrosses and Mollymawks
Genus *Diomedea*

Northern Royal Albatross *Diomedea epomophora sanfordi* (Toroa). 120–130 cm.

Habitat and distribution: Ranges throughout subantarctic seas. Occurs off coasts of Cook Strait and South Island during breeding season. Nesting on Taiaroa Head, Otago.

Characteristics: This subspecies is slightly smaller than the Southern Royal Albatross, *D. epomophora epomophora*. Sexes similar in size.

Voice: Bill clapping and hoarse screams during breeding season.

Food: Squid and surface fish.

Breeding: Nest every second year after they reach age of 8 or 9 years. Single white egg laid in late October in nest constructed of grasses and small sods of earth. Both parents incubate for spells of 4–8 days. Incubation period 11 weeks and chick fledges when 36 or 37 weeks old. Period from egg-laying to fledging of chick averages 45 weeks.

Left: Northern Royal Albatross on nest.
Right: Two Royal Albatrosses in flight.

Royal Albatross, showing wings with long forearms.
Immature Royal Albatross, courtship display.

Genus *Diomedea*

White-capped (Shy) Mollymawk *Diomedea cauta.* 90–100 cm.
Buller's Mollymawk *Diomedea bulleri.* 75–80 cm.

Habitat and distribution: Inhabit South Pacific Ocean up to about 35° latitude. Buller's Mollymawk also ranges to coasts of Peru and Chile.

Characteristics: The White-capped is the largest of the mollymawks. Both species can be seen in seas around Stewart Island, where they often follow fishing boats.

Voice: Silent except on breeding grounds.

Food: Squid and surface fish. Also scavenge for offal from fishing boats.

Breeding: Northern subspecies of Buller's Mollymawk (*D.b.platei*) nests in small numbers on the Three Kings Islands, but other species nest on southern outlying islands and the Chatham Islands.

White-capped (Shy) Mollymawk.

24

White-capped (Shy) Mollymawks in flight.
Northern Buller's Mollymawk.

Family PROCELLARIIDAE: Shearwaters, Diving Petrels, Prions and Gadfly Petrels
Genus *Puffinus*

Flesh-footed Shearwater *Puffinus carneipes* (Toanui). 45 cm.
Buller's Shearwater *Puffinus bulleri.* 46 cm.

Habitat and distribution: Flesh-footed Shearwaters inhabit warmer waters of northern New Zealand and, together with Buller's Shearwater, can be seen from boats in the Hauraki Gulf. Buller's Shearwaters migrate to the North Pacific after the nesting season.

Characteristics: Buller's Shearwater is easily recognised by the 'W' marking on the upper wings. Flesh-footed Shearwaters often dive for baited fishing lines.

Voice: Silent except on nesting grounds, Flesh-footed Shearwaters utter a repeated 'coo-coo-ah' when approaching nesting area. Buller's Shearwaters have a braying call.

Food: Both species take squid and fish. Flesh-footed Shearwaters also take fish offal from boats.

Breeding: Flesh-footed Shearwaters nest on offshore islands as far south as Cook Strait. Buller's Shearwaters nest only on the Poor Knights Islands. Both species are summer nesters, laying a single white egg in a burrow. Both sexes incubate.

Buller's Shearwaters, showing distinctive upper wing pattern.

Flesh-footed Shearwater.

Genus *Puffinus*

Sooty Shearwater *Puffinus griseus* (Titi). 43 cm.

Habitat and distribution: This species, the main 'muttonbird' of the Maori, is very numerous in New Zealand seas, particularly around Stewart Island. Many migrate to the North Pacific after breeding.

Characteristics: New Zealand's commonest breeding bird, the Sooty Shearwater is seen off our coasts singly, or more commonly in very large rafts.

Voice: Sometimes cackle when feeding. At breeding grounds the Sooty Shearwater utters a repeated 'coo-ah', ending with 'krek'.

Food: Small squid, fish and krill.

Breeding: Nests in burrows on many offshore islands and on the mainland on Banks and Otago peninsulas. Very large numbers on islands off Stewart Island. Single white egg laid in late November. Both sexes incubate for an average of 52 days.

Sooty Shearwater.

A flock of Sooty Shearwaters.
Sooty Shearwaters.

Genus *Puffinus*

Fluttering Shearwater *Puffinus gavia* (Pakaha). 33 cm.
North Island Little Shearwater *Puffinus assimilis haurakiensis.*
30 cm.

Habitat and distribution: Fluttering Shearwater inhabits coastal waters from Marlborough Sounds northwards. Little Shearwater is confined to northern coastal waters.

Characteristics: The Little Shearwater is smaller and has a darker back than the Fluttering Shearwater. Both have a rapid wingbeat interspersed with short glides.

Voice: Silent except on breeding grounds. Fluttering Shearwater utters repeated 'car-hek', ending with a slurred note. Little Shearwater has a higher-pitched, cackling 'wa-ee'.

Food: Small fish and crustaceans captured by diving from the surface.

Breeding: Fluttering Shearwaters nest in burrows on offshore islands from Marlborough Sounds to Northland. Little Shearwaters nest on islands off the coast of northern New Zealand.

Hutton's Shearwater *Puffinus huttoni,* which nests in burrows high on the Seaward Kaikoura Mountains, is almost identical to the Fluttering Shearwater. It is slightly larger and its plumage appears darker.

North Island Little Shearwater.

Genus *Pelecanoides*

Common Diving Petrel *Pelecanoides urinatrix urinatrix (Kuaka).*
20 cm.

Habitat and distribution: Occurs throughout the year in coastal waters of North and South Islands.

Characteristics: Recognised by its rapid, whirring flight, skimming close to the surface, often plummeting to dive.

Voice: Usually silent. On breeding grounds this petrel utters repeated wailing 'kuaka' (Maori name) and chattering sounds.

Food: Dives for small fish and krill.

Breeding: Nests in burrows in soft soil on many offshore islands, from Three Kings in the north to Stewart Island. Often visits breeding grounds throughout the year. A single egg is laid from August to October (in south).

PHOTO D.W. HADDEN

Common Diving Petrel.
A flock of Fluttering Shearwaters.

31

Genus *Procellaria*

Black Petrel *Procellaria parkinsoni.* 46 cm.

Habitat and distribution: Ranges far out to sea in the Pacific Ocean and Tasman Sea. Usually only seen in inland waters during the nesting season.

Characteristics: Distinguished from the commoner Flesh-footed Shearwater by stronger flight and black-tipped bill.

Voice: A rapidly repeated 'clack-clack' on breeding ground, but usually silent when flying in at night.

Food: Is thought to catch squid at night.

Breeding: Largest colony nests in burrows on Great Barrier Island. Smaller numbers on Little Barrier Island. One white egg laid early December.

Black Petrel.

PHOTO D.O.C. C.R. VEITCH

Genus *Procellaria*

Westland Petrel *Procellaria westlandica.* 51 cm.

Habitat and distribution: Confined to coastal seas from Cape Egmont to Foveaux Strait, also on east coast from East Cape to Banks Peninsula.

Characteristics: Is the largest of the burrowing petrels and shearwaters. When swimming, it floats high on the water.

Voice: Silent at sea and when flying into nesting grounds. Repeated shrieking after landing.

Food: Mainly squid, but also feeds on offal from fishing trawlers.

Breeding: Nests in burrows in hills of Westland south of the Punakaiki River, laying one egg in May.

Westland Petrel.

PHOTO D.O.C. C.R. VEITCH

Genus *Daption*

Cape Pigeon *Daption capense*. 40 cm.

Habitat and distribution: Common in coastal waters during winter and spring, especially off South Island coasts. Often observed from inter-island ferries.

Characteristics: This species is unmistakable, as its wing pattern is unlike any other petrel or shearwater.

Voice: A chattering call when feeding.

Food: Small squid, fish and krill.

Breeding: Does not nest on New Zealand mainland or offshore islands. Nests in Antarctic regions and Snares Islands.

Cape Pigeon.

Genus *Macronectes*

Northern Giant Petrel *Macronectes halli*. 80–90 cm.

Habitat and distribution: Common around our southern coasts. Often seen from inter-island ferries in Cook Strait. Frequents northern waters in winter.

Characteristics: Large size. Distinguished from mollymawks by prominent nostril tube extending along its heavy bill.

Voice: Guttural sounds when feeding, silent on the wing.

Food: Squid, fish and offal from fishing boats.

Breeding: Does not nest on mainland. Builds a cup-shaped nest and lays a single egg in early spring on many subantarctic islands.

Northern Giant Petrel.

Genus *Pachyptila*

Fairy Prion *Pachyptila turtur* (Titi-wainui). 23 cm.

Habitat and distribution: Common in all coastal waters. Usually seen in large flocks.

Characteristics: The Fairy Prion's blue-grey plumage camouflages it with the sea. The bird does not usually alight on the water except to feed. Usually seen in loose flocks.

Voice: Silent at sea, but makes cooing and grating sounds on nesting grounds.

Food: Small surface fish, krill and plankton.

Breeding: Very large numbers nest in burrows, rock crevices and caves on Stephens Island in Cook Strait. Also breed on many other offshore islands. Single white egg laid in October or November.

Fairy Prion.

PHOTO D.W. HADDEN

Genus *Pachyptila*

Broad-billed Prion *Pachyptila vittata* (Parara). 28 cm.

Habitat and distribution: Occurs in all coastal waters but commonest in the south.

Characteristics: Widest part of bill equals head width. This species is recognised by habit of flocks skimming over water surface when feeding, swinging their heads from side to side while immersing their large bills in water to extract crustaceans.

Voice: Silent at sea but cooing and grating sounds at nesting grounds.

Food: Plankton.

Breeding: Nests in burrows on islands around Stewart Island. Very large numbers nest in the Chathams. Single white egg laid August to September.

Right: Newly fledged Broad-billed Prion chick.
Below: Broad-billed Prion.

Genus *Pterodroma*

Pycroft's Petrel *Pterodroma pycrofti.* 28 cm.

Habitat and distribution: Mainly inhabits waters off east coasts of North Island.

Characteristics: An endangered species. Smaller and a little darker than Cook's Petrel, from which it is difficult to distinguish when flying.

Voice: High-pitched 'zip-zip' repeated when coming in to land. Also subdued cooings.

Food: Not known. Probably small cephalopods.

Breeding: Nests in burrows on islands off the east coast of Northland and in Mercury Bay.

Pycroft's Petrel. Many petrels have to launch themselves into the air from high points, such as trees or cliffs. They have difficulty taking off from the ground due to their long wings.
Below: Pycroft's Petrel.

Genus *Pterodroma*

Cook's Petrel *Pterodroma cookii* (Titi). 30 cm.

Habitat and distribution: Inhabits seas off east coasts of New Zealand but also seen in the Tasman Sea. After breeding migrates to eastern Pacific Ocean.

Characteristics: Typical 'gadfly' flight. Recognised by light-coloured head and neck and white underparts. Difficult to distinguish from Pycroft's Petrel in flight.

Voice: A bleating, rapid 'kek-kek-kek' call when flying overland in rainy weather and over nesting site.

Food: Feed at night on cephalopods, small fish and crustaceans.

Breeding: Main nesting area is Little Barrier Island. Small numbers also nest on Great Barrier Island and Codfish Island off Stewart Island.

Cook's Petrel.

Genus *Pterodroma*

Grey-faced Petrel *Pterodroma macroptera gouldi* (Oi). 41 cm.

Habitat and distribution: Common in seas around the North Island. Ranges far out to sea. Does not migrate.

Characteristics: Usually occurs singly. Distinguished by its large size, dark plumage and grey face. When disturbed from resting on the water, rises effortlessly and soars in wide arcs.

Voice: When coming in to breeding grounds utters repeated 'ooi', also 'kek-kek'.

Food: Feeds at night on zooplankton and probably fluorescent organisms.

Breeding: Nests in winter on most of the North Island offshore islands, also on North Island scrub- and low-forest-covered headlands. One white egg is laid in burrow in late June or July. Both sexes incubate for spells of several days, for a total period of 55 days.

A newly fledged Grey-faced Petrel chick.

Family OCEANITIDAE: Storm Petrels
Genus *Pelagodroma*

White-faced Storm Petrel *Pelagodroma marina maoriana* (Takahi-kare-moana). 20 cm.

Habitat and distribution: Common around coasts of New Zealand. After breeding, many migrate to coasts of Ecuador and Peru.

Characteristics: This species is recognised by very small size and eratic flight, appearing to bounce off the surface with feet dangling.

Voice: At nesting site a twittering 'tiu-tiu-tiu'.

Food: Zooplankton and small crustaceans.

Breeding: In burrows and rock crevices on many small islands and islets off coasts of North and South Islands. One white egg with small red spots is laid in November or early December. Incubation shared for 40–45 days.

A flock of White-faced Storm Petrels.
New Zealand White-faced Storm Petrel.

Order SPHENISCIFORMES: Penguins
Family SPHENISCIDAE: Penguins
Genus *Megadyptes*

Yellow-eyed Penguin *Megadyptes antipodes* (Hoiho). 76 cm.

Habitat and distribution: Occasionally seen in seas of Cook Strait. More commonly on coasts of Canterbury, Otago, Southland and Stewart Island.

Characteristics: A timid and wary species, this is the world's rarest penguin. It usually comes ashore late in the day. Sexes similar.

Voice: Trumpeting and trilling calls.

Food: Squid and fish.

Breeding: Nests in clumps of flax, scrub and forest close to shore, often in a scrape lined with grasses, against a tree trunk or log. Nests are always hidden away from other nesting pairs. One or two white eggs are laid in September to December. Both sexes incubate in turn for 40–50 days. Chicks fledge when 15 weeks old.

Yellow-eyed Penguin and chick.

42

Genus *Eudyptes*

Fiordland Crested Penguin *Eudyptes pachyrhynchus* (Pokotiwha).
71 cm.

Habitat and distribution: Occurs around coasts of South
Westland, Fiordland and Stewart Island. In summer months
stragglers occur in northern waters.

Characteristics: The most timid species of penguin. Slightly smaller
than the Yellow-eyed Penguin.

Voice: Trumpeting, short barks and hisses.

Food: Fish, squid and krill.

Breeding: Nest in rock crevices or hollows beneath tree roots in
coastal forests in Fiordland and especially on Codfish Island. Two
white eggs laid in August. Both sexes incubate for spells of several
days. Incubation period 32–35 days. Chicks fledge when 10 or 11
weeks old.

Fiordland Crested Penguin.

PHOTO D.O.C. A. MUNN

Genus *Eudyptula*

Blue Penguin *Eudyptula minor* (Korora). 40 cm.

Habitat and distribution: Common around coastal waters from North Cape to Stewart Island. Usually seen singly or in small groups.

Characteristics: The smallest species of penguin. Swims low in water and dives when disturbed. Comes ashore at night to roost or when nesting. On the Canterbury coast a race of blue penguins have white edges to their flippers. These 'white-flippered' penguins interbreed with normal Blue Penguins and are not now considered to be a subspecies.

Voice: Moans and a subdued quack uttered offshore before coming to land. During breeding season moans and high-pitched wails and screams.

Food: Small fish and crustaceans.

Breeding: Nest in rock crevices, caves, beneath tree roots and in burrows. The nests are often a considerable distance from shore. In the north 2 white eggs are laid from July to January; in southern regions laying is from September to November. Both sexes incubate for 33–40 days. Chicks fledge when 7 or 8 weeks old.

Blue Penguins.

Blue Penguin and nest in a cave.
Blue Penguin.

Order PELECANIFORMES: Gannets and Cormorants
Family SULIDAE: Gannets and Boobies
Genus *Morus*

Australasian Gannet *Morus serrator* (Takapu). 91 cm.

Habitat and distribution: Common and increasing in numbers in seas around all New Zealand coasts, especially around the North Island. Juveniles migrate to Australian waters and return when 4 years old to nest in New Zealand natal colonies.

Characteristics: Sexes similar. Large size and white wings with black trailing edges distinguish it from other seabirds. Dives from 20 or 30 metres, or shallow dives in surf to capture fish. Often sits on surface.

Voice: Silent except when nesting. Repeated 'awah-awah' when coming in to land. Also quacks and croaks.

Food: Live fish captured by diving to depths of up to 15 metres in open sea. Shallow dives in surf or when catching surface fish.

Breeding: Nest in large colonies on many islands around the coast. Mainland colonies at Cape Kidnappers, Muriwai, Pelorus Sound and Farewell Spit. One white egg laid from early September to December. Both sexes incubate for 42–44 days. Chicks fledge when 16 weeks old.

Australasian Gannet.

Australasian Gannet.
Australasian Gannets diving for fish.

Family PHALACROCORACIDAE: Cormorants and Shags
Genus *Phalacrocorax*

Black Shag (Black Cormorant) *Phalacrocorax carbo novaehollandiae* (Kawau). 88 cm.

Habitat and distribution: A cosmopolitan species. Common on inland lakes and sheltered coasts.

Characteristics: Our largest shag or cormorant. Often seen perched on a rock in lakes, or in flocks on sandspits and shellbanks in marine habitats. Flies with alternate wingbeat and glides.

Voice: Raucous guttural calls at nesting sites, otherwise silent.

Food: Feeds on live fish, especially eels, and crustaceans. Fish swallowed head first.

Breeding: Nests during many months of the year in colonies on ledges of cliffs or on the ground on small islands, also sometimes in trees. Clutch of 3 or 4 chalky white eggs is incubated by both sexes for 28–30 days. Chicks fledge when 7 weeks old.

Black Shag (Black Cormorant).

Black Shags.
Black Shag on nest.

49

Genus *Phalacrocorax*

Pied Shag *Phalacrocorax varius varius* (Karuhiruhi). 81 cm.

Habitat and distribution: Frequents sheltered coastal waters, especially in northern regions. Occasionally seen on inland freshwater lakes.

Characteristics: A large, confiding shag, and easily approached compared with other shag species. Perches on rocks or posts with wings spread to dry. Groups perch in cliffside trees.

Voice: Silent except when nesting. Guttural croaks and gurgling sounds.

Food: Live fish, especially eels and flounder.

Breeding: Usually nest in small colonies in cliffside trees. Trees are defoliated by these birds and often die. Nest composed of sticks. Egg laying takes place mainly from September to October, and another peak period in autumn. Clutch of 3 or 4 chalky eggs is incubated by both sexes for 27–30 days. Chicks fledge when 7 or 8 weeks old, but are fed by parents for several more weeks.

Pied Shag (Pied Cormorant) drying wings.

Pied Shag.
Pied Shags and nest.

Genus *Phalacrocorax*

Little Black Shag *Phalacrocorax sulcirostris*. 61 cm.

Habitat and distribution: Inhabits freshwater lakes and sheltered coastal waters. Uncommon in the South Island.

Characteristics: Often seen in groups. Its long narrow bill and glossy plumage distinguishes it from black-plumaged immature Little Shag.

Voice: Croaking and clicking sounds when fishing. Whistles and croaks at nest.

Food: Small fish, crustaceans and insects. Often several birds fish in a pack; birds in the rear leapfrog to front of pack.

Breeding: Small colonies nest in trees or bushes near water, often in association with Little Shags. Nests are of sticks. Peak laying periods in spring and autumn. Clutch of 3 or 4 pale blue eggs with chalky covering. Both sexes incubate; period uncertain.

A nesting colony of Little Black Shags.

Little Black Shags.
Little Black Shags fishing in a pack.

Below: Little Black Shags (Little Black Cormorants).

Genus *Phalacrocorax*

Little Shag *Phalacrocorax melanoleucos brevirostris* (Kawaupaka).
56 cm.

Habitat and distribution: Coastal waters throughout New
Zealand. Also common on inland lakes and wetlands. Often fishes
on small farm ponds and ditches.

Characteristics: A dimorphic species with various plumage phases.
White-throated form commonest. Some pied forms have black or
yellowish smudges on breast. Small head crest sometimes evident.

Voice: Croaks, clucks and coos at nest sites, otherwise silent.

Food: Fish, especially eels, crustaceans and insects. Does not fish in
packs as does Little Black Shag.

Breeding: Nests in small colonies in trees and low bushes, usually
near water. Nest of sticks and grasses. Clutch of 3 or 4 pale-blue eggs
with chalky covering is laid from August to March. Both sexes
incubate.

Smudgy plumage phase of Little Shag.

Little Shags nesting. Bird in pied plumage phase on left.
Little Shag, white-throated plumage phase.

Genus *Leucocarbo*

New Zealand King Shag *Leucocarbo carunculatus*. 76 cm.

Habitat and distribution: Inhabits coastal waters on southern side of Cook Strait.

Characteristics: One of the rarest shags in the world. Recognised by being the only pink-footed shag in the Cook Strait region.

Voice: Not studied.

Food: Dives from surface for variety of fish.

Breeding: Time of nesting varies from year to year. Nest built of iceplants, seaweed, grasses and sticks on bare, sloping rocks close to the water. Two pale blue eggs with chalky covering.

King Shag.

PHOTO D.O.C. A. COX

Genus *Leucocarbo*

Stewart Island Shag *Leucocarbo chalconotus.* 68 cm.

Habitat and distribution: Inhabits coastal waters from Otago Peninsula south to Stewart Island.

Characteristics: A dimorphic species. Occurs in pied and dark-plumaged phases. Dark phase commonly called 'bronze shag'. Displays head crests during early breeding season.

Voice: Barks and cackles at nest sites.

Food: Fish and crustaceans captured by diving from the surface.

Breeding: Nesting season varies from year to year. A very substantial nest of sticks, seaweed and other plants is built on sloping rock platforms on islets and headlands. Clutch of 2 or 3 pale blue eggs with a chalky covering.

Stewart Island Shags, bronze and pied plumage phases.

Genus *Stictocarbo*

Spotted Shag *Stictocarbo punctatus punctatus* (Parekareka). 73 cm.

Habitat and distribution: Common in coastal waters of Hauraki Gulf and Auckland's west coast. Also found in Wellington Harbour, Marlborough Sounds, Banks Peninsula and Otago Peninsula.

Characteristics: A slender-bodied shag, recognised by black spots on back and prominent double head crests during breeding season.

Voice: Grunts and guttural sounds when nesting, otherwise silent.

Food: Dives from surface for variety of fish and crustaceans. Often ranges far out to sea to fish.

Breeding: An early nester. In the north a nest of sticks and weeds is built in June in caves or on rock ledges, often on steep cliff faces. Clutch of 2 or 3 eggs are pale blue with a chalky covering. Both sexes incubate for 28–30 days.

Spotted Shag. This bird has no nuptial crests.

Spotted Shags.
Below left: A cliff face nesting colony of Spotted Shags.
Below right: Spotted Shag and nest.

Order CICONIIFORMES: Herons, Bitterns and Egrets
Family ARDEIDAE: Herons and Bitterns
Genus *Ardea*

White-faced Heron *Ardea novaehollandiae novaehollandiae*. 66 cm.

Habitat and distribution: Recently self-introduced from Australia, this species is now common throughout New Zealand on sheltered sea coasts, estuaries, harbours, inland lakes and open farmland.

Characteristics: Slimmer than marine Reef Heron. Prominent white face and dark trailing edge to wings in flight. Often occur in large flocks during winter, especially on mudflats.

Voice: Guttural croaks.

Food: Wide range of small fish, crustaceans, frogs, tadpoles, earthworms and insects. Has habit of raking with foot to disturb invertebrates in tidal pools.

Breeding: Nests as early as June or July in northern districts. Favourite site is in pine trees, macrocarpa or large pohutukawa trees. Nest of sticks, often flimsy, contains 2–4 pale turquoise-coloured eggs. Both sexes incubate for 24–26 days. Chicks fledge when 6 weeks old.

White-faced Heron.

White-faced Heron in flight.
White-face Heron, nest and chicks.

Genus *Egretta*

White Heron *Egretta alba modesta* (Kotuku). 91 cm.

Habitat and distribution: A cosmopolitan species. Less than 200 birds live in New Zealand. Inhabit wetlands, open country with streams, tidal lagoons.

Characteristics: During breeding season adults grow long nuptial plumes and their yellow bills turn black. The largest of the heron species. As with other herons, the neck is folded back in flight.

Voice: Guttural sounds and croaks when nesting, otherwise silent.

Food: Small fish, eels, frogs, tadpoles and crustaceans.

Breeding: The only New Zealand nesting site is on the banks of the Waitangiroto River in Westland. Here, in low trees, a colony of 47 pairs (1990) begin egg-laying from late September to November. A clutch of 2–5 pale-blue eggs is laid in a nest constructed of sticks. Both sexes incubate for 24–26 days. Chicks fledge when 6 weeks old.

White Heron.

White Heron.
Pair of White Herons at nest.

Genus *Egretta*

Reef Heron *Egretta sacra sacra* (Matuku moana). 66 cm.

Habitat and distribution: Frequents rocky shores and tidal inlets. Only rarely seen in freshwater habitats.

Characteristics: Recognised by its overall slate-grey colour. Build more stocky and bill heavier than White-faced Heron.

Voice: Guttural croaks when disturbed or at nest.

Food: Small fish, especially small flounder, crustaceans and mud crabs.

Breeding: Nests are built of sticks on rock ledges in caves or rock crevices, also in clumps of flax or in hollows under roots of coastal pohutukawa trees. A nest is often added to and used year after year. Two or three pale turquoise-coloured eggs are laid from September to January. Both sexes incubate for 25–27 days. Chicks fledge when 5½–6 weeks old.

Reef Heron.

Above left: Reef Heron feeding
chick at nest in a cave.
Right: Reef Heron fishing with
spread wing attitude.

Reef Herons.

Genus *Egretta*

Little Egret *Egretta garzetta nigripes.* 56 cm.

Habitat and distribution: A few birds migrate from Australia during autumn and winter to feed on tidal estuaries and harbours in northern areas. Also occasionally seen in South Island.

Characteristics: Smaller size than White Heron. Bill and legs black. 'Dances' actively when feeding in shallow water. Not usually seen in freshwater habitats.

Voice: Silent.

Food: Small fish, crustaceans and insects.

Breeding: Not recorded as nesting in New Zealand.

The smaller sized Little Egret as compared with Black-backed Gull.

Genus *Nycticorax*

Nankeen Night Heron *Nycticorax caledonicus.* 56 cm.

Habitat and distribution: Frequents tidal estuaries and mangrove swamps.

Characteristics: Recognised by its overall chestnut colouring and squat appearance. Usually perches in trees during daytime and feeds mainly at night.

Breeding: In recent years several pairs have nested in trees near the banks of the Wanganui River.

Nankeen Night Heron, a rare straggler to New Zealand.

Genus *Bubulcus*

Cattle Egret *Bubulcus ibis coromandus.* 51 cm.

Habitat and distribution: A late-autumn and winter migrant to New Zealand from Australia. Usually seen feeding around cattle for the disturbed insects and earthworms. Sometimes observed in tidal estuaries.

Characteristics: Recognised by its stocky build, buff crown and neck in late spring. Usually seen in flocks. Wary. Has a rapid wingbeat when compared with other herons.

Voice: Silent.

Food: Insects, grubs and earthworms.

Breeding: Our birds return to New South Wales to nest in November. Not yet recorded as nesting in New Zealand.

Cattle Egrets.

Cattle Egrets.

Genus *Botaurus*

Australasian Bittern *Botaurus poiciloptilus.* 71 cm.

Habitat and distribution: Wetlands, swamps, especially when overgrown with reeds and raupo. Also occasionally seen among mangroves.

Characteristics: Usually seen singly. When disturbed, either crouches low or points bill upward and freezes. Well camouflaged in raupo. Flight slow, with neck folded as with herons.

Voice: Low guttural croaks. Male utters low booming call in breeding season from late August to early summer. More frequently heard in evening. Female utters watery bubbling call when approaching nest.

Food: Freshwater fish, especially eels, frogs, tadpoles and insects. Reported to occasionally take small birds and mice.

Breeding: Female alone builds bulky nest of raupo and rushes in dense vegetation. She lays 3–6 olive-brown eggs at 2-day intervals. Incubation starts with laying of second egg. Female alone incubates for 24–26 days. Chicks are fed by regurgitation; they leave nest and wander in surrounding vegetation when about 10 days old, and can fly when 5 weeks old.

Australasian Bittern at nest.

Australasian Bittern fishing in swamp.
Australasian Bittern, showing camouflage.

Family THRESKIORNITHIDAE
Genus *Platalea*

Royal Spoonbill *Platalea regia* (Kotuku ngutu-papa). 78 cm.

Habitat and distribution: Usually seen in small groups feeding at water's edge in lagoons, tidal estuaries and mudflats. Many non-breeding juveniles inhabit the Vernon Lagoons in Marlborough and the Manawatu River estuary throughout the year.

Characteristics: Recognised by large size, white plumage and black, spoon-shaped bill. Unlike herons, the Royal Spoonbill flies with neck extended. Often flies and soars in wide arcs.

Voice: Bill clapping and low grunts when nesting, otherwise silent.

Food: Feeds in shallow water, swinging bill from side to side to capture small fish and crustaceans.

Breeding: A few pairs nest high in kahikatea trees near the White Heron colony in Westland. Others nest on the ground on small, low islands in the Vernon Lagoons. Recently some have nested on Maukiekie Island, Otago, and on Green Island near Dunedin. A bulky nest of sticks is lined with grasses. A clutch of 2–4 whitish eggs with brown speckles is laid October–December. Both sexes incubate for 22–25 days. Chicks fly when 7 weeks old.

Royal Spoonbill.

Royal Spoonbills fly with necks outstretched, unlike herons.
Pair of Royal Spoonbills at nest.

Order ANSERIFORMES: Swans, Geese and Ducks
Family ANATIDAE: Swans, Geese and Ducks
Genus *Cygnus*

Mute Swan *Cygnus olor* 150 cm.

Habitat and distribution: Introduced to New Zealand in 1860s, they inhabit Lake Ellesmere in small numbers. Also a few birds on several small lakes.

Characteristics: Conspicuous large white bird. Flies with neck outstretched.

Voice: A hiss and subdued low whistle.

Food: Shoots of water plants, also aquatic invertebrates.

Breeding: Nest in stands of dense raupo. Clutch of 4–10 white eggs laid from September to November. Incubation, only by female, for 35 days.

Mute Swans.

Genus *Cygnus*

Black Swan *Cygnus atratus.* 130 cm.

Habitat and distribution: Introduced as a game bird from Australia in the 1860s, these swans are very numerous on Lake Ellesmere, Rotorua lakes, Vernon Lagoons and several urban-park lakes. Also found in some marine habitats such as northern Kaipara Harbour.

Characteristics: Black body. In flight, white wing-tips are conspicuous.

Voice: Trumpet, hiss and whistle.

Food: Shoots of water plants and some invertebrates. Also come ashore to graze pastures.

Breeding: Nest built of reeds and vegetation in stands of raupo and lakeside vegetation. Often nest as early as June in the north, and through to December. Clutch of 4–10 eggs is incubated by both sexes for 35 days.

Black Swans and cygnets.

Genus *Branta*

Canada Goose *Branta canadensis maxima.* 100 cm.

Habitat and distribution: Introduced to New Zealand in 1905, this species inhabits South Island high-country lakes and Lake Ellesmere. It was recently introduced to North Island.

Characteristics: Often seen on high-country pastures in South Island. Fly in a 'V' formation.

Voice: Hoarse honking and trumpeting.

Food: Graze vegetation and eat seeds. Graze farm pastures and cause fouling.

Breeding: Main nesting area is near headwaters of South Island rivers east of the Southern Alps. Nest of grasses lined with down is built in vegetation and 2–10 white eggs are laid from late September to November. Female alone incubates these for 30 days.

Canada Geese.

Genus *Cereopsis*

Cape Barren Goose *Cereopsis novaehollandiae.* 85 cm.

Habitat and distribution: First introduced to Otago in 1914, but the population died out. Now seen as stragglers from Australia. Frequents open-country wetlands.

Characteristics: Recognised by overall grey colour, long legs and erect posture.

Voice: Repeated honking when in flight.

Food: Grazes grasses and other vegetation, also eats seeds.

Breeding: No recent nest records for New Zealand. Breeds in Australia.

Cape Barren Geese, female incubating on nest.

Genus *Tadorna*

Chestnut-breasted Shelduck *Tadorna tadornoides*. 65 cm.

Habitat and distribution: This Australian species has been seen in New Zealand in increasing numbers during recent years. Similar in size to the Paradise Shelduck, it is distinguished by a white neckband and white around the eye of the female. Has not been recorded as nesting in New Zealand to date.

Chestnut-breasted Shelducks.

PHOTO D.W. HADDEN

Genus *Tadorna*

Paradise Shelduck *Tadorna variegata* (Putangitangi). 63 cm.

Habitat and distribution: Widely distributed throughout New Zealand in open country and inland lakes. Also found in high altitude streams.

Characteristics: Usually seen in pairs in open country, also in flocks on lakes. Male has overall dark plumage, female is conspicuous for her white head.

Voice: A vocal bird when in flocks. A high-pitched honk is made by the male when disturbed.

Food: Graze pastures, eat lake weeds, seedheads of grasses, also insects and earthworms.

Breeding: Birds pair for life. They nest in rock crevices, hollow logs, rabbit burrows, or under exposed tree roots. The nest of grasses is lined with down feathers. Clutch of 6–12 white eggs is laid from August to October. Incubation, only by female, for 31 days.

Above left: Paradise Shelduck, female.
Above right: Paradise Shelduck, male.
Below: Paradise Shelduck ducklings.

Genus *Hymenolaimus*

Blue Duck *Hymenolaimus malacorhynchos* (Whio). 53 cm.

Habitat and distribution: An endemic threatened species, the Blue Duck inhabits turbulent high-country rivers of North and South Islands. Does not occur north of central North Island. Recent introductions have been made to some rivers of Mt Taranaki.

Characteristics: The only duck species likely to be seen on turbulent high-country rivers. Soft fleshy borders to bill. Usually very well camouflaged when perched on river rocks. Strong, direct flight.

Voice: Male gives repeated high-pitched whistle. Female utters low rasping note when disturbed.

Food: Insects and grubs taken from surface or around rocks. Caddis-fly larvae a favourite food.

Breeding: Nests from August to December. Nest constructed of sticks and grasses hidden under rocks, in caves, under logs or in thick riverside vegetation. Clutch of 4–8 cream-coloured eggs is incubated for 32 days only by the female. Chicks can fly when 10 weeks old.

Pair of Blue Ducks.

Blue Duck in typical habitat.
Blue Duck with seven ducklings.

Genus *Anas*

Mallard *Anas platyrhynchos platyrhynchos*. 58 cm.

Habitat and distribution: Inhabits shallow-water ponds and lakes, also saltwater estuaries, lagoons and mudflats throughout New Zealand.

Characteristics: Introduced to New Zealand for game purposes from Europe and America, the Mallard comprises 80 per cent of our dabbling ducks. The female is somewhat similar to the Grey Duck, but is distinguished by a blue or purple speculum and orange-coloured legs.

Voice: Females quack, males utter subdued 'guab-guab-guab'.

Food: Vegetable matter, seeds, insects, grubs and earthworms.

Breeding: In poolside vegetation nests are built with grasses and lined with down. A clutch of 8–12 buff-coloured eggs is laid from August to January, and incubated by female for 28 days.

Mallard, female showing purple speculum.

Mallard in flight.
Mallard pair.

Genus *Anas*

Grey Duck *Anas superciliosa superciliosa* (Parera). 55 cm.

Habitat and distribution: Inhabits shallow freshwater rivers, streams, lagoons and alpine tarns. Occasionally seen in tidal estuaries.

Characteristics: Duck and drake have similar plumage. Distinguished from female Mallard by white underwing and green speculum. In recent years numbers have been reduced by competition with introduced Mallard.

Voice: Similar to Mallard. Female a quack, male utters soft 'guab-guab'.

Food: Vegetable matter and seeds. Insects, snails and earthworms.

Breeding: In northern regions, nests as early as June, but usually August to December. Nest of grasses is lined with down, usually sited in rank vegetation but some nests are built several metres above ground in hollows or forks of trees. Clutch of 6–10 cream-coloured eggs is incubated by female for 27 or 28 days.

Grey Duck, female, showing green speculum.

Grey Duck, pair.
Grey Duck and ducklings.

Genus *Anas*

Grey Teal *Anas gracilis* (Tete). 43 cm.

Habitat and distribution: Inhabits shallow lagoons and freshwater lakes which provide good shore cover. A mobile species, many arriving from Australia.

Characteristics: Grey Teal show conspicuous white triangle on upper wing when in flight. Speculum is bluish-green.

Voice: Female utters repeated rapid quack, male a hoarse rasping.

Food: Shoots of water plants, insects and earthworms.

Breeding: Nest of grasses is built in tree hollows, rabbit burrows or niggerheads. Clutch of 6–8 cream-coloured eggs is laid from June to January and incubated by female for 24–26 days. Grey Teal readily accept artificial nest-boxes.

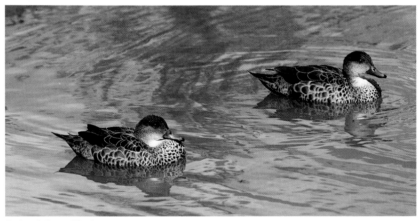

Pair of Grey Teal.
Grey Teal, showing white and green speculum.

Genus *Anas*

Brown Teal *Anas aucklandica chlorotis* (Pateke). 48 cm.

Habitat and distribution: Brown Teal is an endangered endemic species. Main population is in wetlands on Great Barrier Island, others found in Northland on brackish, slow-flowing rivers. Prefers habitats with heavy vegetation on banks. Breeds well in captivity.

Characteristics: Brown Teal are usually seen in small flocks which do not readily fly off when disturbed but swim away.

Voice: Female a rapid repeated quack, male a hoarse rasping.

Food: Shoots of water plants, invertebrates and insects.

Breeding: Nest of grasses is lined with down and built in dense vegetation near water. Clutch of 4–8 buff-coloured eggs is laid during many months of the year but mainly July to January. Female incubates for 27–30 days.

Brown Teal.

Genus *Anas*

New Zealand Shoveler *Anas rhynchotis variegata* (Kuruwhengi).
48 cm.

Habitat and distribution: Inhabits lowland swamps and shallow lake edges. Often found in tidal harbours and off the coast during shooting season. Uncommon in Stewart Island.

Characteristics: Recognised by its wedge-shaped bill which has lamellae along edges for filtering food from ooze. The Shoveler is our fastest flying duck. Conspicuous white wing-bar in flight.

Voice: Usually fairly silent. Female gives a soft quack.

Food: Seeds, insects and earthworms.

Breeding: Nests of grasses lined with down are built in thick vegetation near water. Clutch of 6–10 cream-coloured eggs with blue tinge is laid from August to December. Incubation by female for 26 days.

New Zealand Shoveler, camouflaged.

New Zealand Shoveler, female.
New Zealand Shoveler, male.

Genus *Aythya*

New Zealand Scaup *Aythya novaeseelandiae* (Papango). 40 cm.

Habitat and distribution: Inhabits clear-water lakes and lagoons, including mountain lakes. Not usually seen on shallow wetlands.

Characteristics: New Zealand's only true diving duck. Dives and remains submerged for 20 seconds or more. Conspicuous white wing-bar visible in flight. Usually seen in small flocks sitting on water.

Voice: Females utter a subdued quack, males a low whistle.

Food: Dives for small fish and eats invertebrates and surface insects.

Breeding: Nests composed of grasses and lined with down are built in thick vegetation close to water. Clutch of 5–8 cream-coloured eggs laid from October to January. Incubation by female for 28 days.

New Zealand Scaup, male.

New Zealand Scaup, female with ducklings.
Group of New Zealand Scaup.

Order FALCONIFORMES: Diurnal birds of prey
Family ACCIPITRIDAE: Hawks
Genus *Circus*

Australasian Harrier *Circus approximans* (Kahu). 60 cm.

Habitat and distribution: Widely distributed in open country throughout New Zealand and hunts along borders of forests. Non-breeding birds roost at night in communal roosts in sedge and raupo.

Characteristics: Leisurely flight compared with Falcon. Quarters the ground with slow wingbeat and glides in search of prey. Perches on posts.

Voice: Usually silent. During nesting season utters high-pitched 'kee-kee'.

Food: Large insects, lizards, frogs, birds and rodents. Occasionally catches fish and tadpoles. Frequently feeds on carrion, especially possums killed on road.

Breeding: In northern areas may nest as early as August, but usually October to November. Bulky nest of sticks, grasses and rushes is built in raupo swamps, clumps of pampas and occasionally in crown of tree fern. Incubation of 3 or 4 buff-coloured eggs by female takes 29–32 days. Incubation starts after laying of first egg so chicks are disproportionate in size and youngest chick seldom survives. Chicks fly when 6 weeks old.

Australasian Harrier.

Australasian Harrier eating carrion.
Australasian Harrier and nest.

Family FALCONIDAE: Falcons
Genus *Falco*

New Zealand Falcon *Falco novaeseelandiae* (Karearea). 45 cm.

Habitat and distribution: Eastern race inhabits South Island high country, the southern race Fiordland. The Bush Falcon inhabits forested regions of Westland and the North Island. Falcons are rarely found north of the central North Island.

Characteristics: Rapid flight and long tail distinguish it from the larger Australasian Harrier. Female is markedly larger than male.

Voice: Rapid repeated 'kek-kek-kek', also a subdued high-pitched scream, especially in immature birds.

Food: Large insects, lizards and rodents. Main diet appears to be smaller passerine birds, especially starlings, skylarks and finches.

Breeding: Falcons use no nesting material. Eggs are laid in a depression on the ground under overhanging rocks, fallen logs or on ledges of rocky bluffs. Bush Falcons also reported to occasionally nest in clumps of perching epiphytes.

Clutch of 3 eggs are buff, heavily blotched with dark russet-brown markings. Laying takes place from September to December. Incubation is by both sexes for 30–33 days. Chicks are fed by female with food captured by the male. The smaller male chicks fly when 32 days old and female chicks when 35 days old.

New Zealand Falcon at nest.

Above: Immature New Zealand Falcon.
Centre: New Zealand Falcon in flight.
Bottom: New Zealand Falcon, head, showing tubercle in nostril and dark eye.
Right: New Zealand Falcon.

Order GALLIFORMES: Game birds
Family PHASIANIDAE: Partridges, Quails and Pheasants
Genus *Callipepla*

California Quail *Callipepla californica brunnescens.* 25 cm.

Habitat and distribution: Introduced to New Zealand in the 1860s and now found throughout the country in scrub and open land. Often seen in coveys.

Characteristics: Prominent head crest in male, smaller crest in female. Runs rapidly and flies with rapid wingbeat.

Voice: Calls 'Miss Harper' or 'tobacco'.

Food: Seeds and fruits of many plants, also shoots, leaves and a few insects.

Breeding: Nests from September to February. Nest composed of grasses hidden under log or in dense vegetation, often under fallen manuka or gorse. Clutch of 10–18 cream-coloured eggs, blotched and streaked with light brown, is incubated by hen for 23 days.

California Quail.

Genus *Alectoris*

Chukor *Alectoris chukar.* 33 cm.

Habitat and distribution: Chukor were introduced to New Zealand in 1920s. They inhabit high, dry, rocky country in the South Island east of the Alps.

Characteristics: Overall grey plumage with conspicuous black and white bars on flank.

Food: Mainly seeds, shoots, leaves and berries.

Voice: A repeated 'chuck-chuck'.

Breeding: Nest of grasses under rock or in thick vegetation. Clutch of 10–20 cream-coloured eggs with purple blotches is laid from September to January. Female incubates for 24 days.

Chukor.

Genus *Synoicus*

Brown Quail *Synoicus ypsilophorus.* 18 cm.

Habitat and distribution: Introduced to New Zealand from Australia in 1860s. Found only in North Island, particularly Northland. Inhabits open country with scrub.

Characteristics: Recognised by small size, dumpy appearance and overall brown colour. Usually seen in coveys. Rapid flight.

Voice: Long whistle, with rising inflection.

Food: Seeds, clover, shoots and leaves, fruits and insects.

Breeding: Nest of grasses is sited on ground in thick herbage. Clutch of 6–12 eggs is laid from September to December. Eggs, off-white colour with brown speckles, are incubated by hen for 21 days.

Brown Quail.

Genus *Phasianus*

Ring-necked Pheasant *Phasianus colchicus.* 60–80 cm.

Habitat and distribution: Introduced to New Zealand in the 1840s, this pheasant is common in the north of North Island in scrub, open country and farmland. Apart from in the Nelson region, it is not common in South Island.

Characteristics: Long tail and bright colours, unlike other game birds. Ring-necked Pheasants interbreed with the introduced Black-necked variety. Hen is of overall brown colour and has a shorter tail.

Voice: Cock bird utters three-syllable 'croork', with rustle of wings.

Food: Seeds, fruits, green shoots and leaves and insects.

Breeding: Polygamous. Male accompanies 3 or 4 females. The nest of grasses is built in thick vegetation. 6–14 olive-brown eggs are laid from September to January and incubated by hen for 23 days.

Ring-necked Pheasant, male.

Order GRUIFORMES: Rails
Family RALLIDAE: Rails and Coots
Genus *Rallus*

Banded Rail *Rallus philippensis assimilis* (Moho-pereru). 30 cm.

Habitat and distribution: Inhabits mangrove swamps, salt marshes and wetlands; also follows streams into farmlands. Found mainly north of Bay of Plenty, also Northwest Nelson and Stewart Island.

Characteristics: Often seen running rapidly among mangroves. Although a strong flier, appears reluctant to take to the air when disturbed.

Voice: High-pitched, penetrating squeak; low growling and grunting sounds near nest.

Food: Crustaceans, insects and earthworms.

Breeding: In northern districts nesting starts in August; probably double-brooded, as nesting as late as February has been recorded. Nests of sedges and grasses are built in salt-marsh sedges or thick herbage. Clutch of 2–5 buff-coloured eggs with dark brown blotches is incubated for 18 or 19 days by both sexes.

Banded Rail on nest.

Right: Banded Rail approaching nest.
Below: Banded Rail.

Genus *Gallirallus*

North Island Weka *Gallirallus australis greyi.* 53 cm.
Western Weka *Gallirallus australis australis.*
Stewart Island Weka *Gallirallus australis scotti.*

Habitat and distribution: Wekas inhabit a wide range of habitats: open country with scrub, forest margins, sand dunes and rocky shores. North Island Wekas are found in Northland, Poverty Bay and on Kapiti Island. Western Wekas inhabit Marlborough, Nelson, Westland and Fiordland. The Stewart Island subspecies was introduced to Kapiti Island.

Characteristics: Most active at dusk, Wekas are flightless, swim well and have a strong homing instinct. Western and Stewart Island subspecies are dimorphic, with dark-plumaged forms being common in Fiordland.

Voice: A repeated drawn out 'ee-wee' with a rising inflection.

Food: Eats a wide range of invertebrates, seeds, fruit and lizards; also robs eggs and young from ground-nesting birds and petrel burrows, and has been reported as taking mice and rats.

Breeding: Nesting throughout year, with peak period from September to November. Nest of dry grasses in hollow under logs or rocks, or in thick vegetation. Clutch of 2–5 cream-coloured eggs with dark brown blotches. Incubation by both parents for 25 or 26 days.

North Island Weka and nest.

North Island Weka.
Western Weka.

Genus *Porzana*

Spotless Crake *Porzana tabuensis plumbea* (Puweto). 20 cm.

Habitat and distribution: Inhabit swamps throughout New Zealand. Even small pockets of raupo and swamp often harbour a few birds.

Characteristics: Seldom seen in the open. Very secretive and crepuscular in habit. Readily responds to tape-recorded calls.

Voice: A rattling warble and repeated musical 'dook-dook'.

Food: Insects, grubs, earthworms and tadpoles.

Breeding: Commonest nest site is in clump of small cutty grass within a raupo swamp. The nest, composed of grasses and reeds, is usually sited half to 1 metre above water level. Clutch of 2 or 3 dark buff-coloured eggs with dark markings are laid from August to November. Both sexes incubate for 19–22 days.

Spotless Crake at nest.

Genus *Porzana*

Marsh Crake *Porzana pusilla affinis* (Koitareke). 18 cm.

Habitat and distribution: Inhabit swamps throughout New Zealand. More common in South Island, rare in Northland.

Characteristics: Secretive and crepuscular in habit. Often flies short distance when flushed. Responds to tape-recorded calls. Browner than Spotless Crake.

Voice: Soft purring and 'kek-kek' calls.

Food: Insects and other invertebrates.

Breeding: Few nests have been found in New Zealand. Some have been located in tussock sedge near lake edge.

Marsh Crake and nest.

PHOTO D.W. HADDEN

Genus *Porphyrio*

Pukeko *Porphyrio porphyrio melanotus.* 51 cm.

Habitat and distribution: Common in wetter areas throughout New Zealand. Inhabits swamps, lake edges and pastures which have clumps of rushes.

Characteristics: In some areas birds live as communities, others have been seen in pairs. In spite of clumsy flight, can fly long distances. Swims well.

Voice: Raucous high-pitched screech; subdued, musical 'tuk-tuk'.

Food: Mainly feeds on vegetable matter. Shoots are held in foot, parrot fashion. Also feeds on invertebrates and robs eggs from nests.

Breeding: Single pairs nest in raupo swamps or in clumps of rushes in paddocks or rank grass. In communities, two or more females lay in one nest and incubation is shared by several birds. The nest is composed of grasses and rushes. Single pairs lay from 3–6 buff-coloured eggs with dark spots and blotches; communal birds may incubate up to 12 eggs. Pukekos nest during many months of the year, but usually August to January. Incubation period is 24 days.

Pukeko at nest with newly hatched chick.

Above left: Pukeko, showing large feet.
Above right: Pukeko swimming.
Below: Pukekos feeding two-week-old chick.

Genus *Porphyrio*

South Island Takahe *Porphyrio mantelli hochstetteri*. 63 cm.

Habitat and distribution: Wild population confined to mountains west of Lake Te Anau in tussock and remnants of beech forest. Birds introduced to Kapiti, Maud and Tiritiri Matangi Islands where they are breeding.

Characteristics: Recognised by heavy build and thick bill. Is flightless, although possessing wings. In 1998 wild population approximately 160 birds and 40 on islands.

Voice: Somewhat similar to weka call, with rising inflection. Often call in duet. Other calls a low 'klomph'.

Food: Feeds mainly on succulent shoots and basal stems of red tussock, also seeds and berries. In winter feeds on rhizomes of ferns in beech forests.

Breeding: Nest is built of grasses in bower of tussock clumps. Two buff-coloured eggs with brown markings are laid in October or November. Both sexes incubate for 30 days. Usually only one chick survives and is fed by its parents until the following September.

Head of South Island Takahe.

Chewed Tussock stems – signs of Takahe feeding.
Pair of South Island Takahe.

Genus *Fulica*

Australian Coot *Fulica atra australis.* 38 cm.

Habitat and distribution: Self-introduced from Australia in 1958, this coot is now found throughout New Zealand in freshwater lakes which have a fringe of raupo or reeds.

Characteristics: The most aquatic of the rail family, this bird seldom comes ashore. Flies strongly. Often seen in flocks after nesting season.

Voice: A penetrating, reed-like 'kraak'.

Food: Feeds mainly on vegetable matter such as shoots from water plants, also invertebrates.

Breeding: Nest, constructed of reed stems and raupo, is built in cover of reed beds or on low willow branches trailing in water. Clutch of 3–6 cream-coloured eggs with dark spots is laid from August to January. Both sexes incubate for 21–23 days. Two or more broods are raised each season.

Australian Coots.

Pair of Australian Coots at nest.
Australian Coot feeding chicks.

Order CHARADRIIFORMES: Waders, Gulls and Terns
Family HAEMATOPODIDAE: Oystercatchers
Genus *Haematopus*

South Island Pied Oystercatcher *Haematopus ostralegus finschi*
(Torea). 46 cm.

Habitat and distribution: Throughout the year non-breeding birds
inhabit estuaries, mudflats and sheltered beaches. In autumn and
winter these are joined by birds which have bred, forming very large
flocks. During the breeding season birds inhabit South Island
farmland, riverbeds and subalpine regions.

Characteristics: Usually seen in flocks of several thousand birds
resting on shellbanks and sandspits at high tide. Uniform pied
marking and slimmer build distinguish it from larger Variable
Oystercatcher.

Voice: Musical high-pitched 'tu-eep'. In breeding season a repeated
rippling 'ku-vee-ku-vee-ku-vee', ending in quieter notes.

Food: Marine crustaceans, molluscs, bivalves, marine worms and
occasionally small fish. On farmland the birds feed on insects and
other invertebrates and earthworms.

Breeding: South Island Oystercatchers are thought to pair for life.
Until recent report from Hawke's Bay it was believed they nest only
on South Island riverbeds, pastures and ploughed land. Nest is a
scrape in ground in which 2 or 3 buff-coloured eggs with brown
blotches are laid from August to October. Both sexes incubate for
24–27 days.

South Island Pied Oystercatcher.

Flock of South Island Pied Oystercatchers.
South Island Pied Oystercatcher and nest on riverbed.

Genus *Haematopus*

Variable Oystercatcher *Haematopus unicolour* (Torea; dark phase, Torea pango). 48 cm.

Habitat and distribution: Inhabits rocky shores and sandy ocean beaches throughout New Zealand. Usually observed in pairs, but flocks of 50 or more birds seen in winter months. Not seen inland (c.f. South Island Pied Oystercatcher).

Characteristics: A polymorphic species, occurring in black, pied and intermediate phases. Only black birds occur in Stewart Island.

Voice: Musical high-pitched 'tu-eep'. During courtship utters repeated rippling 'ku-vee'.

Food: Marine crustaceans, worms and bivalves, especially tuatua, which are placed on end in sand and prised open.

Breeding: Nest is a scrape in sand, on dunes or near driftwood. On rocky coasts it is often sited on a rock ledge or in sand between rocks. Clutch of 2 or 3 large buff-coloured eggs, heavily marked with dark brown, incubated by both sexes for 27 or 28 days.

Pair of Variable Oystercatchers at nest.

Variable Oystercatchers.
Pied plumage phase of Variable Oystercatcher.

Family RECURVIROSTRIDAE: Stilts
Genus *Himantopus*

Australasian Pied Stilt *Himantopus himantopus leucocephalus* (Poaka). 38 cm.

Habitat and distribution: Occupies wide range of habitats — wet open pastures, wetlands, lagoons, estuaries and mudflats — throughout North and South Island. Rare on Stewart Island.

Characteristics: Distinguished from Pied Oystercatcher by smaller body, black bill and very long legs which extend well behind tail when flying. Increasing in numbers, and often seen in large flocks.

Voice: A repeated high-pitched 'yep-yep'.

Food: In marine habitats these stilts feed on crustaceans and molluscs. In fresh water or farmlands their prey is insects and earthworms.

Breeding: Pied Stilts nest in loose colonies, with nests 10 metres or more apart. In wet paddocks nesting starts in July or August. In sand dunes or shellbanks nesting extends from September to December. A clutch of 2–4 brown eggs, heavily marked with dark-brown or black blotches, is laid in a scrape in the ground lined with varying amounts of nesting material. Incubated by both sexes for 24–26 days.

Australasian Pied Stilt and nest.

Pied Stilts in flight.
Ten-day-old Australasian Pied Stilt.

Below: Newly hatched Australasian Pied Stilt chicks.

Genus *Himantopus*

Black Stilt *Himantopus novaezelandiae* (Kaki). 38 cm.

Habitat and distribution: A very endangered species now confined to the Waitaki River system in Otago. Found in swamps and beside freshwater lagoons and riverbeds. In winter a few birds migrate to northern harbours.

Characteristics: Long legs and totally black plumage of adults. Immature birds are partially pied. Hybridises with Pied Stilt.

Voice: Repeated high-pitched 'yap-yap'.

Food: Insects and their larvae and earthworms.

Breeding: Unlike Pied Stilts, Black Stilts nest in isolation and are vulnerable to predation. The nest is a scrape in shingle, lined with few grasses. 2–4 brown eggs, blotched with black are laid from September to November and incubated by both sexes for 25 days.

Black Stilt.

Hybrid Black Stilt with Australasian Pied Stilts.
Immature Black Stilt.

Family CHARADRIIDAE: Dotterels and Plovers
Genus *Charadrius*

New Zealand Dotterel *Charadrius obscurus* (Tuturiwhatu). 27 cm.

Habitat and distribution: This threatened species occurs north of eastern Bay of Plenty and Raglan, also in Stewart Island. In winter some birds move to Farewell Spit. Prefers sandy beaches.

Characteristics: Well camouflaged when seen on sandy beaches. Runs rapidly and circles when flying. Russet-coloured breast in breeding plumage. Call is often heard before bird is sighted.

Voice: Call is a single 'prip', and a high-pitched 'pweep' when disturbed.

Food: Crustaceans, molluscs and worms. On sand dunes takes sandhoppers and insects.

Breeding: Nests on sand dunes or near pieces of driftwood on beach. The nest, a scrape in sand, sometimes lined with a little dry grass, is often found under pingao or marram grass, also on shellbanks. In Stewart Island nests are sited on rocky highlands. A clutch of 2 or 3 buff-coloured eggs with dark-brown blotches are laid from August to December. Incubation, mainly by female, takes 28–30 days.

New Zealand Dotterel on nest.

New Zealand Dotterel, winter plumage.
New Zealand Dotterel, summer plumage.

Genus *Charadrius*

Banded Dotterel *Charadrius bicinctus bicinctus* (Tuturiwhatu). 18 cm.

Habitat and distribution: Inhabits sandy beaches, mudflats, salt marshes, open short-grass paddocks, riverbeds and high country, e.g. Rangipo Desert. Many birds migrate to Australia in autumn when others move to coastal estuaries.

Characteristics: Our commonest plover. After nesting and moult, birds congregate to feed in flocks. Their double breast-bands are then absent. Runs rapidly. In flight narrow white wing stripe is visible.

Voice: A high-pitched 'pit-pit' and a vibrating 'churr'.

Food: Insects, small crustaceans and molluscs; earthworms when feeding on farm paddocks.

Breeding: Nest in scrape in soil or shingle with little or no nest material. On shingle riverbeds nest is often lined with lichen or moss. The Banded Dotterel also nests on sand dunes. Its usual clutch of 3 brown or grey eggs with dark-brown blotches is laid from August to December. Both sexes incubate for 26 or 27 days.

Male Banded Dotterel.

Pair of Banded Dotterels at nest on river bed.
Banded Dotterel nesting on sand dune.

Genus *Charadrius*

Black-fronted Dotterel *Charadrius melanops.* 18 cm.

Habitat and distribution: Self-introduced from Australia, probably about 1950s. Now established on rivers of Hawke's Bay, Wairarapa and Manawatu. In South Island have colonised rivers in Marlborough, Canterbury, Otago and Southland.

Characteristics: Smaller than Banded Dotterel. Conspicuous white wing patch in flight, which is undulating. Well camouflaged on shingle riverbeds when it turns its back to intruder.

Voice: A repeated 'pit-pit' and a rippling 'cree-ee'.

Food: Invertebrates and earthworms.

Breeding: Nest a mere scrape among river shingle. Clutch of 3 or 4 buff-coloured eggs with dark blotches is laid from September to February. Both sexes incubate for 25 or 26 days.

Black-fronted Dotterel at nest.

Newly hatched Black-fronted Dotterel chicks.
Black-fronted Dotterel incubating on nest.

Genus *Anarhynchus*

Wrybill *Anarhynchus frontalis* (Ngutuparore). 20 cm.

Habitat and distribution: During nesting season most birds move to the shingle riverbeds of Canterbury and Otago. After nesting, most move north to spend autumn and winter on mudflats and estuaries in the North Island.

Characteristics: Very easily approached when in flocks, the Wrybill is easily recognised by its unique bill with its tip bent to right. Runs rapidly and well camouflaged against river shingle. Flocks fly in tight formation, twisting and turning.

Voice: A subdued chattering in flocks, a 'sweet' call in flight.

Food: Feeds on insects, their larvae and spiders. On mudflats Wrybill has distinctive feeding method by swinging bill sideways to capture marine organisms from ooze.

Breeding: Nests on shingle riverbeds in Canterbury and Otago. A clutch of 2 pale-grey eggs with dark spots is laid in scrape between river stones from August to October. Late nests may be built in December if early nests lost through flooding. Both sexes incubate for 29 or 30 days.

Wrybills.

126

Wrybills.
Below left: Wrybill.
Below right: Wrybill and nest on riverbed.

Genus *Arenaria*

Turnstone *Arenaria interpres.* 23 cm.

Habitat and distribution: Migrate to New Zealand, arriving in late September, and leave in late March. Usually seen in small flocks resting on shellbanks at high tide or feeding on rock platforms. On mudflats and stony beaches this species turns over seaweed and stones in search of prey.

Characteristics: Tortoiseshell plumage colour and short legs distinguish the Turnstone from other migrant waders. Flock often fly off very suddenly when approached.

Voice: A vibrating 'tit-tit' when flushed.

Food: Insects and crustaceans.

Breeding: Nests in tundra regions of Alaska and Siberia.

Turnstones.
Turnstones in flight.

Genus *Pluvialis*

Pacific Golden Plover *Pluvialis fulva.* 25 cm.

Habitat and distribution: Migrate to New Zealand in small numbers in early summer, leaving in late March. Usually seen on mudflats and coastal short-grass paddocks. Often roost with Turnstones.

Characteristics: Pacific Golden Plovers are usually seen in eclipse plumage when they are well camouflaged on mudflats. They are similar in size to New Zealand Dotterel but slimmer. The **Grey Plover**, *Pluvialis squatarola*, visits New Zealand in smaller numbers. It is slightly larger and can be distinguished by its whitish tail and black axillaries.

Voice: In flight gives melodious, clear, repeated double whistle.

Food: Crustaceans, molluscs and insects.

Breeding: Nests in tundra regions of Alaska and Siberia.

Pacific Golden Plover.

Genus *Vanellus*

Spur-winged Plover *Vanellus miles novaehollandiae.* 38 cm.

Habitat and distribution: Self-introduced to Southland from Australia in 1930s. Now inhabits open-country pastures, riverbeds, shorelines of lakes and sheltered coasts throughout New Zealand.

Characteristics: Recognised by black head with prominent yellow wattles, long legs and lapwing flight.

Voice: A loud rattling call.

Food: Insects, grubs and earthworms, also marine crustaceans.

Breeding: Nest as early as June in northern regions, with later broods in November and December. Nest is a depression in ground lined with few grasses, in paddocks or stony ground. Lays 2–4 dark-brown heavily blotched eggs. Incubation shared by sexes for 30 days.

Spur-winged Plovers and nest.

A flock of Spur-winged Plovers.
A Spur-winged Plover chick.

Family SCOLOPACIDAE: Sandpipers, Godwits and Curlews
Genus *Calidris*

Lesser Knot *Calidris canutus canutus* (Huahou). 25 cm.

Habitat and distribution: Migrant from Northern Hemisphere, arriving New Zealand late September and starting on return migration in late March. Inhabits mudflats, estuaries and sandspits, often in association with Godwits. Some non-breeding birds over-winter in New Zealand.

Characteristics: After the Godwit this is second most numerous wader. Half size of Godwit and shorter bill and legs.

Voice: Muted chattering when roosting.

Food: Crustaceans, molluscs and marine worms.

Breeding: Nests in tundra regions of Siberia.

Lesser Knots in flight.

Lesser Knot, nuptial plumage.
Lesser Knot, eclipse plumage.

133

Genus *Calidris*

Curlew Sandpiper *Calidris ferruginea.* 22 cm.

Habitat and distribution: Arrives in New Zealand in late September from Northern Hemisphere. Return migation commences late March and April. Inhabits estuaries, mudflats and sandspits. Often associates and roosts with Wrybills or Banded Dotterels.

Characteristics: Recognised by decurved bill. At high tide roosts with Wrybills. Spectacular russet-coloured nuptial plumage assumed in February or March. White wing stripe and upper tail coverts evident when in flight.

Voice: Sometimes gives musical liquid 'chirrip' when disturbed.

Food: Feeds by probing deeply for marine worms, molluscs and crustaceans. In Australia reported to feed on seeds.

Breeding: Nests in tundra regions of Siberia.

A Curlew Sandpiper with Wrybills.

134

Curlew Sandpiper, eclipse plumage.
Curlew Sandpiper, nuptial plumage.

Genus *Calidris*

Sharp-tailed Sandpiper *Calidris accuminata. 22* cm.
Pectoral Sandpiper *Calidris melanotos. 22* cm.

Habitat and distribution: Migrants from Northern Hemisphere. Arrive in New Zealand late September, with return migration in April. Found in small groups on salt marshes, lagoons and mudflats. Pectoral Sandpipers are less common and prefer brackish and freshwater habitats near shore.

Characteristics: The Sharp-tailed Sandpiper has boomerang-shaped brown markings on sides of breast and sometimes a chestnut-coloured crown. The Pectoral Sandpiper has darker markings with more prominent demarcation between breast and white underparts.

Voice: Usually silent, but both species sometimes give a double 'whitt' whistle when flushed.

Food: Both species feed on insects and their larvae on shallow pools. Sharp-tailed Sandpipers also feed on marine organisms on mudflats.

Breeding: Both species nest in tundra regions of Northern Siberia.

Sharp-tailed Sandpipers.

136

Sharp-tailed Sandpipers with Wrybills.
Pectoral Sandpipers.

Below: Pectoral Sandpipers.

137

Genus *Calidris*

Red-necked Stint *Calidris ruficollis*. 15 cm.

Habitat and distribution: Migrant from Siberia, arriving New Zealand late September and returning late March or April. Inhabits mudflats and estuaries. Roosts with Wrybills at high tide.

Characteristics: The smallest of the migrant waders, the Red-necked Stint is a little larger than a sparrow and markedly smaller than the Wrybill. Often assumes russet-coloured 'balaclava' in February or March.

Voice: Sometimes gives high-pitched 'wit-wit' when flushed.

Food: Pecks very rapidly with 'sewing machine' action, to feed on small marine organisms.

Breeding: Nests in tundra regions of Siberia.

Red-necked Stint, nuptial plumage.

Red-necked Stints with Wrybills.
Red-necked Stint with New Zealand Dotterel, illustrating size.

139

Genus *Numenius*

Eastern Curlew *Numenius madagascariensis*. 61 cm.
Asiatic Whimbrel *Numenius phaeopus variegatus*. 41 cm.

Habitat and distribution: Small numbers of Curlew and Whimbrel migrate to New Zealand from Siberia, arriving in late September and returning in late March. Both species inhabit estuaries, mudflats and lagoons throughout New Zealand.

Characteristics: Both species are wary and difficult to approach. The Curlew is our largest migrant wader, recognised by its very long decurved bill. The Asiatic Whimbrel is Godwit-sized but has a bill distinctly decurved.

Voice: Curlew has musical, flute-like warbling ('quee-quee'), the Whimbrel a higher-pitched rippling whistle.

Food: Both species feed on marine crustaceans, molluscs and marine worms. Mud crabs are a common source of food.

Breeding: Both species nest in tundra regions of Siberia.

Two Eastern Curlews with South Island Pied Oystercatchers and Lesser Knots in flight.

140

Eastern Curlew.
Asiatic Whimbrel.

Genus *Limosa*

Eastern Bar-tailed Godwit *Limosa lapponica baueri* (Kuaka). 40 cm.

Habitat and distribution: Up to 100,000 godwits migrate to New Zealand from Eastern Siberia and Alaska, arriving late September and returning in late March or early April. Some immature birds over-winter in northern New Zealand. They inhabit mudflats, estuaries and coastal lagoons throughout, but greatest concentrations are at Farewell Spit and in northern harbours.

Characteristics: Females are larger and have longer bills. Males assume russet-coloured nuptial plumage before return migration. Small number of **Black-tailed Godwits**, *Limosa limosa*, are seen among flocks of Bar-tailed Godwits. These can be recognised by their straighter bills and more uniform colouring. They show a conspicuous white wing-bar and white upper-tail coverts in flight.

Voice: A twittering double 'tuu-tuu' note in roosting flocks, also 'kwit-kwit' in flight.

Food: Probe deeply in mud for wide range of marine worms, crustaceans and molluscs.

Breeding: Nest in Eastern Siberia and Alaska.

Eastern Bar-tailed Godwits in flight.

Eastern Bar-tailed Godwit, nuptial plumage.
Eastern Bar-tailed Godwit, eclipse plumage.

Genus *Tringa*

Wandering (Alaskan) Tattler *Tringa incana.* 28 cm.
Siberian (Grey-tailed) Tattler *Tringa brevipes.* 25 cm.

Habitat and distribution: A small number of Tattlers visit New
Zealand from the Northern Hemisphere from late September to
April. Wandering Tattlers prefer rocky shores and shingle beaches.
Siberian Tattlers inhabit mudflats and estuaries and often roost with
Wrybills at high tide.

Characteristics: These two species are difficult to differentiate in the
field. The Wandering Tattler is slightly the larger and this bird's
nasal groove extends for two-thirds length of bill; Siberian Tattler's
extends half way along bill. This feature only seen at very close
quarters. In breeding plumage, the barred underparts extend to
under-tail coverts in the Wandering Tattler.

Voice: Wandering Tattler gives a rippling trill of several notes; the
Siberian Tattler utters a high-pitched two-note whistle.

Food: Small fish, crustaceans and other marine organisms.

Breeding: Both species nest in tundra regions of North-eastern
Siberia.

Siberian (Grey-tailed) Tattler.

Siberian (Grey-tailed) Tattler with Wrybills.
Wandering (Alaskan) Tattler.

Genus *Tringa*

Terek Sandpiper *Tringa terek.* 23 cm.

Habitat and distribution: Small numbers of this species migrate to New Zealand in late September. They feed on mudflats and estuaries and leave at end of March. Terek Sandpipers often rest with Wrybill flocks at high tide.

Characteristics: Easily recognised by its upturned bill. White trailing edge to wing evident in flight. A restless bird.

Voice: In flight a musical trill, but usually silent.

Food: Often probes deeply for marine worms and crustaceans; also feeds on insects and their larvae in shallow, brackish pools.

Breeding: Breeds in tundra regions from Finland to Siberia.

Terek Sandpiper, eclipse plumage.
Terek Sandpiper, nuptial plumage.

Genus *Tringa*

Marsh Sandpiper *Tringa stagnatilis.* 25 cm.

Habitat and distribution: Small numbers visit New Zealand from late September to April. They prefer brackish and freshwater pools near coast.

Characteristics: A slim, very active sandpiper. Often associates with Pied Stilts. Recognised by lightish colour and thin bill, compared with other sandpipers.

Voice: Usually silent, but repeated single 'twee' when flushed.

Food: Mainly insects and their larvae, also crustaceans.

Breeding: Nests in Central Eurasia.

Marsh Sandpiper (right) with Pied Stilt.

Family STERCORARIIDAE: Skuas
Genus *Catharacta*

Brown (Subantarctic) Skua *Catharacta skua lonnbergi* (Hakoakoa). 63 cm.

Habitat and distribution: Inhabits southern coasts and offshore islands of Stewart Island. After nesting, often forms flocks at sea.

Characteristics: A large, aggressive bird somewhat resembling an immature Black-backed Gull. Has hooked beak and white wing patches.

Voice: High-pitched screech when disturbed.

Food: Feeds on carrion and on other seabirds, their eggs and chicks.

Breeding: Nests on offshore islands off Stewart Island from September to December. Nest is a scrape in ground lined with a few grasses and lichens. Two stone-coloured eggs with dark-brown blotches are incubated by both sexes for 30 days.

Brown (Subantarctic) Skua.

Genus *Stercorarius*

Arctic Skua *Stercorarius parasiticus.* 45 cm.

Habitat and distribution: Migrates to New Zealand coastal waters during our summer months. Common in Hauraki Gulf or wherever there is a good White-fronted Tern population.

Characteristics: Is dimorphic. Occurs in dark or light mottled plumage phases. Seen settled on water or chasing terns and gulls.

Voice: Usually silent when in this country.

Food: Pursues White-fronted Terns or Red-billed Gulls, forcing them to disgorge fish. These are caught and eaten in mid-air.

Breeding: Nests in Northern Hemisphere.

Arctic Skua, dark plumage phase.
Arctic Skua.

Family LARIDAE: Gulls and Terns
Genus *Larus*

Black-backed Gull (Dominican) *Larus dominicanus dominicanus*
(Karoro). 60 cm.

Habitat and distribution: Common throughout New Zealand on
open coasts, harbours and estuaries, also inland and often at high
altitudes. Numerous at city refuse dumps.

Characteristics: Our largest gull, and the only one with a black
back. Young in their first year are brown. In second year back is
brown and breast and neck white flecked with brown.

Voice: When disturbed near territory, circles and utters repeated
'ga-ga-ga'. Also has long 'garw-w-w' call.

Food: A wide range of shellfish, crustaceans, molluscs, worms and
insects. Shellfish are often carried high in air and dropped to break
shell. Also eat carrion.

Breeding: Most pairs nest in colonies near seashore, but others nest
in isolation on rocky headlands, islets or inland near lakes, also on
mountainsides at high altitudes. The nest is composed of grasses,
dry seaweed and other dry vegetation. A clutch of 2 or 3 brownish
or grey eggs with dark blotches is laid from late October to
December. Both sexes incubate for 24–26 days.

Southern Black-backed Gull and nest.

Southern Black-backed Gull.
Southern Black-backed Gull on left with immature bird.

Genus *Larus*

Red-billed Gull *Larus novaehollandiae scopulinus* (Tarapunga). 37 cm.

Habitat and distribution: Common throughout New Zealand around coasts, estuaries, and urban parks, but uncommon inland.

Characteristics: Adults easily recognised. Juveniles have brown tips to feathers of back and mantle, dark-brown bill and legs. This bird has a heavier build and thicker bill than the Black-billed Gull.

Voice: High-pitched, raucous 'scrark'.

Food: Small fish, crustaceans and molluscs. These gulls paddle with feet in wet sand to bring up worms. In flooded paddocks they eat earthworms and insects; also rob eggs from White-fronted Terns' nests.

Breeding: Nest in colonies on rocky headlands and islets off coast. A few pairs nest inland with Black-billed Gulls on shore of Lake Rotorua. Nests, close together, are composed of dry grasses and seaweed. In these 2 brown-coloured heavily blotched eggs are laid from September to December. Both sexes incubate for 24–26 days. Red-billed Gulls sometimes interbreed with Black-billed Gulls.

Red-billed Gull.

Immature Red-billed Gull.
Red-billed Gull nesting.

Genus *Larus*

Black-billed Gull *Larus bulleri.* 37 cm.

Habitat and distribution: Inhabits inland lakes, rivers and estuaries. Tends to migrate to coasts in winter months. More common in South Island.

Characteristics: Less confiding to humans than Red-billed Gull. Slimmer build, with noticeably thinner black bill. Immature birds have buff tips to feathers of mantle and back. Outer primary wing feathers have white tips with black edges.

Voice: Similar to Red-billed Gull but quieter.

Food: Insects and their larvae, invertebrates and earthworms. Often follow plough. On coast eat crustaceans and molluscs.

Breeding: Usually nest on inland riverbeds and shores of some lakes. Most nest in South Island. Some small colonies are found on sheltered coastal spits of North and South Island. The nest is often quite substantial, composed of small sticks and grasses. Clutch of 2 brown, heavily blotched eggs is laid in October to December. Both sexes incubate for 22–24 days.

Black-billed Gull and nest.

Black-billed Gulls in flight.
Black-billed Gulls with chicks in creche.

Genus *Sterna*

Black-fronted Tern *Sterna albostriata* (Tarapiroe). 30 cm.

Habitat and distribution: Inhabits riverbeds and farmlands east of the Southern Alps. In autumn most birds migrate to coastal river estuaries in both South and North Islands.

Characteristics: Is noticeably smaller than the common White-fronted Tern, is darker in colour and has orange-coloured bill and feet. Black crown becomes grey and mottled after post-nuptial moult.

Voice: Calls repeatedly with sharp 'tit-tit-tit' when in flight.

Food: Small fish, insects and earthworms. Often seen in flocks hawking insects on inland farm paddocks.

Breeding: Nests on shingle riverbeds of eastern South Island in small loose colonies, with nests 10 or more metres apart. Clutch of 2 or 3 grey eggs with dark-brown blotches is laid in scrape in sand or shingle, from mid October to December. Incubation by both sexes for 21–23 days. Many nests are destroyed by flash floods or predation.

Black-fronted Tern.

Black-fronted Tern and nest on riverbed.
Black-fronted Tern on nest.

Genus *Sterna*

Caspian Tern *Sterna caspia* (Taranui). 51 cm.

Habitat and distribution: Inhabits shallow coastal waters, estuaries and lagoons; sometimes seen in small numbers on inland lakes.

Characteristics: A cosmopolitan species and our largest tern, the Caspian is easily recognised by its heavy body and sickle-shaped wings and tail with shallow fork. On ground, its heavy red bill becomes evident. Black cap becomes grey and speckled after breeding season, and a slight head-crest is sometimes evident.

Voice: A harsh, rasping 'karak'.

Food: Feed only on live fish caught by splashing plunge from 8 to 10 metres above surface.

Breeding: Nest in colonies on shellbanks in harbours or among sand dunes. Some pairs nest in isolation on shingle riverbeds, sandy beaches on small islands, or the shores of lakes. One to three unusually large eggs are laid in a mere scrape in the sand. Both sexes incubate the buff-coloured dark-spotted eggs for 21–23 days.

Caspian Tern colony on an ocean beach.

Caspian Tern in flight.
Caspian Terns. Adult in winter plumage on left, immature bird on right and White-fronted Tern in foreground.

Below: Caspian Terns and chick.

Genus *Sterna*

White-fronted Tern *Sterna striata* (Tara). 42 cm.

Habitat and distribution: Our commonest tern. Inhabits coastal waters throughout New Zealand. Many birds migrate to Australia in autumn but do not nest there. Seldom seen inland.

Characteristics: Distinguished from smaller Black-fronted Tern by general lighter plumage and black bill and feet. Common name of 'kahawai bird' derived from this tern's habit of fishing over surface shoals of these fish.

Voice: A high-pitched repeated 'zitt-zitt'.

Food: Dives for small fish captured just below surface.

Breeding: Nests in colonies on rock headlands and islets, shellbanks and sandy beaches, also on ledges of cliffs. Nests are close together. One or two buff or grey eggs with dark spots are laid on bare ground. Incubation by both sexes for 21 days.

White-fronted Tern colony.

160

White-fronted Tern, adult and newly fledged chick.
White-fronted Tern nesting.

Genus *Sterna*

New Zealand Fairy Tern *Sterna nereis davisae.* 25 cm.

Habitat and distribution: Inhabits a few ocean beaches on east coast of Northland and Kaipara Harbour. Occasionally birds have been seen in Firth of Thames during winter months.

Characteristics: The smallest and rarest of our terns — possibly less than 10 pairs survive. Distinguished from Eastern Little Tern by black eye-stripe ending 5 mm from base of bill, and having no black tip to its yellow bill.

Voice: A high-pitched repeated 'zwit'.

Food: Live small fish caught by a plunging dive.

Breeding: Nests in a scrape in sand, often in a patch of broken shell. Two greyish-buff eggs are laid from November to December and incubated by both sexes for 19 or 20 days.

New Zealand Fairy Tern and nest.

162

Above: New Zealand Fairy Tern in flight.
Below: New Zealand Fairy Terns with chick.

Below: New Zealand Fairy Tern and chicks.

Genus *Sterna*

Eastern Little Tern *Sterna albifrons sinensis.* 25 cm.

Habitat and distribution: Occurs regularly in summer months throughout New Zealand. More common in northern harbours. Some immature birds seen in winter months.

Characteristics: Similar in size to Fairy Tern, but black eye-stripe extends to base of bill. Adult in breeding plumage has yellow bill with black tip.

Voice: Usually silent in New Zealand. Sometimes gives sharp 'zwit' call.

Food: Hovers and dives for small fish.

Breeding: Nests in Asia, New Guinea and Australia.

Eastern Little Tern, breeding plumage.

Eastern Little Tern, eclipse plumage.
Three Eastern Little Terns with White-fronted Terns.

Order COLUMBIFORMES: Pigeons and Doves
Family COLUMBIDAE: Pigeons and Doves
Genus *Hemiphaga*

New Zealand Pigeon *Hemiphaga novaeseelandiae novaeseelandiae* (Kereru). 51 cm.

Habitat and distribution: Widespread throughout forested areas of New Zealand. Also seen in open country when feeding on broom flowers and clover.

Characteristics: Our only endemic species of pigeon. Identified by large size, general greyish-green colour with pure white breast. Pronounced whistling wingbeat.

Voice: A subdued 'goo' or 'ooh'.

Food: Eats a wide range of fruits, seeds, flowers and foliage of native and exotic plants. The New Zealand Pigeon is an important agent for dispersing seed from many plants, especially seeds from podocarp trees.

Breeding: Nesting extends from late August to March. The nest is a flimsy structure of small twigs loosely crossed. The single white egg is often visible from below. Incubation by both sexes takes 29 or 30 days. Clutch overlap may occur, when chick in first nest is attended while a second egg is incubated in a new nest.

New Zealand Pigeon feeding on Nikau fruit.

Right: New Zealand Pigeon in flight.
Centre: New Zealand Pigeon and nest with five-day-old chick.
Bottom: New Zealand Pigeon feeding five-week-old chick.

Genus *Streptopelia*

Barbary Dove *Streptopelia roseogrisea*. 28 cm.

Habitat and distribution: Introduced from North Africa in 1970s, the Barbary Dove inhabits open country with trees, and urban parks in Auckland, Bay of Plenty, Hawke's Bay and Wairarapa.

Characteristics: Pale buff colour with prominent black ring on neck. Often feeds on ground beneath trees.

Voice: A repeated soft 'coo-cruu'.

Food: Seeds, fruits and occasional insects.

Breeding: Flimsy nest of twigs in fork of tree or shrub. There 2 white eggs are laid from August to March. Incubated by both sexes.

Barbary Doves.

Genus *Streptopelia*

Spotted Dove *Streptopelia chinensis tigrina.* 30 cm.

Habitat and distribution: Introduced from Asia. Inhabits open farmland with trees and urban parks. Common around Auckland and spreading to Northern Waikato.

Characteristics: Overall rosy-fawn colour. Strong, low direct flight.

Voice: A repeated 'coo-cruu'.

Food: Seeds, fruits and insects. Large flocks regularly feed on seeds from dried sludge at sewage works.

Breeding: Flimsy nest of fine twigs built in tree fork or shrub. The 2 white eggs, laid from August to March, are incubated by both sexes.

Spotted Doves:

Genus *Columba*

Rock Pigeon *Columba livia.* 33 cm.

Habitat and distribution: Many birds inhabit city parks, others are found in open country with cliffs and rocky terrain for roosting and nesting. Usually seen in small flocks feeding on riverbeds, farmlands or seashore. Introduced from Europe in 1860s.

Characteristics: Colour forms vary from dark grey to light brown or even almost white. Sexes similar.

Voice: Usually only males vocal, uttering a repeated 'coodly-coo'.

Food: Wide variety of seeds, grain from farmlands, legumes, fallen fruits and occasionally insects.

Breeding: Rock Pigeons nest throughout the year, laying 2 white eggs on ledges of rocky cliffs or buildings. Sparse nest material of grasses and small twigs is used. Both sexes incubate for 18 days.

Rock Pigeon.

Rock Pigeons.
Rock Pigeons in a public park.

Order PSITTACIFORMES: Cockatoos and Parrots
Family PSITTACIDAE: Parrots
Genus *Strigops*

Kakapo *Strigops habroptilus.* 63 cm.

Habitat and distribution: This severely endangered species now confined to Codfish Island, with smaller numbers on Maud Island. A small number of male birds may still survive in remote areas of Fiordland. Total population in 1998 is 57 birds.

Characteristics: The largest parrot in the world, with males weighing up to 3 kg. Flightless, although posessing wings which are used to assist balance, nocturnal and usually solitary. Presence in wild shown by chewed tussock stems and leaves.

Voice: Silent except during breeding season when male utters repeated booming calls to attract females for mating in lek behaviour, also piercing screeches and 'ching' calls.

Food: Wide range of foliage, seeds, shoots and rhizomes. Artificial feeding with kumara, apples and nuts is successful.

Breeding: Nest in shallow burrow, beneath tree roots or in hollow log. Nesting only occurs in season when food is plentiful. Clutch of 2–4 white eggs. Incubation and feeding of chicks solely by female.

Kakapo, male.

Above left: Kakapo feeding signs. Fresh chews.
Above right: Dried eight-day-old chews.
Kakapo. The cryptic plumage blends with surrounding ferns.

173

Male Kakapo.

174

Family CACATUIDAE: Cockatoos
Genus *Cacatua*

Sulphur-crested Cockatoo *Cacatua galerita.* 50 cm.

Habitat and distribution: Introduced as cage escapees or self-introduced from Australia. Inhabit open country with small pockets of forest for roosting. Established from Waikato Heads to Raglan, also near Wanganui and in parts of Northern Wairarapa, Manawatu and Wellington Province. Recent reports locate some in Kaipara area, on Northland's west coast and on Banks Peninsula.

Characteristics: Usually seen in flocks feeding on ground, also in trees. Very wary and difficult to approach closely.

Voice: A raucous screech.

Food: Seeds, fruits, buds and leaves, also insects.

Breeding: Nest in tree cavity is usually built high up. Also nests reported in baled haystacks. In Australia the Sulphur-crested Cockatoo is reported to lay 3 or 4 white eggs, which are incubated for 30 days.

Sulphur-crested Cockatoo.

Genus *Nestor*

North Island Kaka *Nestor meridionalis septentrionalis.* 45 cm.

Habitat and distribution: Inhabits large tracts of lowland forest in the North Island and forested offshore islands, but becoming a threatened species on the mainland.

Characteristics: In flight shows rounded wings with scarlet and orange-coloured underwing. Often calls when flying at night. Some birds visit suburban gardens during winter to feed on exotic plants.

Voice: Harsh grating call when disturbed or flying, otherwise soft melodious whistles and warbles. Soft low whistles and chuckles at nest.

Food: Wide range of foliage, shoots, fruits, nectar, insects and their larvae. Strong beak used to rip bark and wood from dead trees in search of grubs.

Breeding: Nest in cavity of mature or dead tree. Clutch of 2–4 white eggs are laid on powdered wood from October to January. Incubation by female, who is fed on the nest every 1½ hours by male. Incubation period 24–26 days. Chicks fledge when 10 weeks old, and are flightless for 2 or 3 days.

North Island Kaka.

North Island Kaka.
North Island Kaka at nest hole.

Male Kaka calling female from nest to feed her.

Genus *Nestor*

South Island Kaka *Nestor meridionalis meridionalis.* 46 cm.

Habitat and distribution: Inhabits forest from Nelson Province, West Coast, Fiordland to Stewart Island.

Characteristics: Slightly larger than North Island subspecies. Greenish tinge and whitish crown.

Voice: Similar calls to North Island Kaka.

Food: Seeds, foliage, shoots, fruits, nectar, insects and grubs.

Breeding: Not studied extensively, but considered similar to North Island Kaka.

A captive South Island Kaka.

Genus *Nestor*

Kea *Nestor notabilis.* 46 cm.

Habitat and distribution: Inhabits South Island high-country forests and mountains.

Characteristics: Olive-green plumage and large hooked beak distinguish it from South Island Kaka. Orange underwing prominent in flight. Confiding, inquisitive and destructive to human belongings.

Voice: High-pitched 'kee-aa' call, especially when flying, also softer murmuring and whistling calls.

Food: Seeds, foliage, fruits, insects and nectar. Also feeds on carrion and attacks sickly sheep.

Breeding: Unlike other parrots, the Kea builds a nest of sticks, grasses, moss and lichens, usually under rock above the bushline or in a forest clearing. Clutch of 2 or 3 white eggs is laid from August to January. Incubation period 23–24 days. Males sometimes mate with two or more females.

Kea.

The bright underwing colour of a Kea.
Kea.

Genus *Platycercus*

Eastern Rosella *Platycercus eximius.* 33 cm.

Habitat and distribution: Introduced to New Zealand from Australia or established from cage escapees. Now common in Northland, Waitakere Ranges, Coromandel, western Waikato, Wairarapa and Upper Hutt Valley. Also in small numbers in Canterbury, Otago and Stewart Island. Inhabits forest and open country close to forests.

Characteristics: Usually seen in pairs or small groups. Flight is rapid and direct.

Voice: Varies with district. Northland birds call with a three-note whistle, with second note lower in pitch. Birds in other areas have a double-note call. Also chatter and babble when feeding.

Food: Wide range of fruits, buds and shoots and flowers. Also feed on seeds of Scotch thistle in paddocks.

Breeding: Nest in cavities in trees, or dead tree fern trunks. One nest was found in hollow strainer post. Clutch of 4–6 white eggs are laid October to January. Incubation by hen for 22–24 days.

The **Crimson Rosella** *Platycercus elegans*, another cage escapee, occurs in small numbers in northwest Wellington and formerly in Dunedin.

Rosella Parakeet at nest hole.

Genus *Cyanoramphus*

Yellow-crowned Parakeet *Cyanoramphus auriceps auriceps* (Kakariki). 25 cm.

Habitat and distribution: Inhabits central forested areas of North Island and Tararua Ranges, also common on many offshore islands. In South Island widespread from Marlborough through Nelson, Westland to Fiordland, also found in parts of Canterbury, Otago and Stewart Island. This species is far more common on the mainland than Red-crowned Parakeet.

Characteristics: Usually seen in small groups, usually high in forest canopy. On offshore islands often forages on ground.

Voice: Rapid 'ki-ki-ki' when in flight; chatters and babbles when feeding.

Food: Seeds, buds and shoots of shrubs, fruits and flowers. Also, in contrast to Red-crowned Parakeet, eats more invertebrates.

Breeding: Nests in cavities in trees, often in end of dead, broken limbs. Clutch of 4–8 white eggs is laid from October to January. Incubated for 20 days by female who is fed by male.

Yellow-crowned Parakeet.

Genus *Cyanoramphus*

Red-crowned Parakeet *Cyanoramphus novaezelandiae novaezelandiae* (Kakariki). 28 cm.

Habitat and distribution: Inhabits lowland native forests. Common on many offshore islands, but becoming increasingly scarce on mainland.

Characteristics: Usually well camouflaged when feeding in broadleaf trees. Red forehead and crown prominent. Often seen in groups. Flight rapid and direct.

Voice: A rapid babbling chatter when feeding. Repeated 'ke-ke-ke' when flying.

Food: Seeds, buds and shoots, flowers, fruits and nectar. Also eat invertebrates but far less than does Yellow-crowned Parakeet.

Breeding: Nest in cavities of trees. On some offshore islands nest in rock crevices on ground. Clutch of 4–9 white eggs is laid from October to January. Incubation for 20 days by female who is called from nest and fed by male at hourly intervals. Male also assists in feeding chicks.

Opposite: Red-crowned Parakeet pair at nest hole, female feeding chick.
Red-crowned Parakeet, male feeding female.

Order CUCULIFORMES: Cuckoos
Family CUCULIDAE: Cuckoos
Genus *Chrysococcyx*

Shining Cuckoo *Chrysococcyx lucidus lucidus* (Pipiwharauroa). 16 cm.

Habitat and distribution: Winters in Solomon Islands, Bougainville and other Pacific Islands in that region. Arrives in New Zealand late September and inhabits forest and open country with trees.

Characteristics: Sparrow-sized, this cuckoo has rapid flight and is well camouflaged in foliage.

Voice: Repeated whistle, each note a rising inflection, followed by descending notes.

Food: Insects and spiders, especially hairy caterpillars.

Breeding: Lays one egg per nest of Grey Warbler. Incubation 12 days. Chick fed by foster parent for several weeks after fledging.

Shining Cuckoo.

Genus *Eudynamys*

Long-tailed Cuckoo *Eudynamys taitensis* (Koekoea). 40 cm.

Habitat and distribution: Winters from Bismarch Archipelago to Marquesa Islands. arrives in New Zealand October. Inhabits forested regions where Whiteheads and Yellowheads live.

Characteristics: Hawk-like appearance. Very long tail is prominent when flying.

Voice: A repeated harsh, hissing screech with a rising inflection. Also a metallic short alarm note.

Food: Insects, grubs and lizards. Is predatory, robbing eggs and chicks from nests. Also reported to have taken small birds and mice.

Breeding: Lays single egg in nest of Whitehead in North Island, and Yellowhead and Brown Creeper in South Island.

Long-tailed Cuckoo in flight.
Long-tailed Cuckoo.

Order STRIGIFORMES: Owls
Family STRIGIDAE: Owls
Genus *Ninox*

Morepork *Ninox novaeseelandiae novaeseelandiae* (Ruru). 29 cm.

Habitat and distribution: Essentially inhabits forests, but adapted to live in open country with clumps of trees for shelter and nesting. Found throughout New Zealand but uncommon in eastern South Island.

Characteristics: Our only endemic owl. Distinguished from introduced Little Owl by dark plumage, rounder head and longer tail.

Voice: Usual call of 'Quor-quo'. Also a vibrating 'cree' and short 'quee' with rising inflection.

Food: Mainly insects, especially moths, wetas and stick insects. Also, small birds, mice and geckos.

Breeding: Nests in tree hollows, clumps of perching epiphytes or in fork of pine tree on bed of pine needles. Two, very occasionally 3, white eggs laid late October or November. Incubation by female for 31 days. Female fed by male. Both parents feed chicks, which fledge when 4½ weeks old.

Morepork with weta.

Morepork flying to nest hole.
Below left: Three-week-old Morepork chicks.
Below right: Morepork at nest hole.

Genus *Athene*

Little Owl *Athene noctua.* 23 cm.

Habitat and distribution: Introduced from Europe in 1906.
Inhabits open country and farmland in South Island. Except in
small pine plantations, does not penetrate forests.

Characteristics: Smaller and squatter than Morepork. Has a low,
bouncing flight. Often seen perched on posts or power poles during
daylight.

Voice: A high-pitched 'tiew' call. Also mewing sounds during
nesting.

Food: Mainly insects and earthworms, also small birds occasionally.

Breeding: Nests in holes in trees, rabbit burrows and stacks of hay
bales. Two to four white eggs incubated by female for 28 days.

Little Owl, pair.

190

Little Owl at nest hole.
Little Owl chick.

Order CORACIIFORMES: Kingfishers
Family ALCEDINIDAE: Kingfishers
Genus *Halcyon*

New Zealand Kingfisher *Halcyon sancta vagans* (Kotare). 24 cm.

Habitat and distribution: Common throughout New Zealand, especially in coastal regions of the northern North Island. Lives in marine habitats, wetlands, open country, farmland and forests. Migrates to coastal areas during winter months.

Characteristics: A wary bird. Often seen perched on rocks, posts, powerlines and trees waiting to capture prey. Male more brightly coloured than female. Russet on flanks and underwing fades in summer.

Voice: Repeated 'kek-kek-kek'. During courtship a vibrating 'kereekeree' with rising inflection. Also short 'krek' when boring.

Food: Insects and their larvae, earthworms, spiders, tadpoles, fish, crabs, freshwater crayfish, skinks, small birds and mice.

Breeding: Bores tunnels in clay banks or rotting tree trunks, or uses cavities in trees. Four or five white eggs laid from November to January. Incubation shared by sexes, but mainly by female. Both parents feed chicks, which fledge when 26 days old. Fed by parents for further 10 days.

New Zealand Kingfisher with skink.

Male Kingfisher feeding newly fledged chick.
A six-week old New Zealand Kingfisher chick.

Genus *Dacelo*

Kookaburra *Dacelo novaeguineae novaeguineae.* 45 cm.

Habitat and distribution: Introduced from Australia. Restricted range from Wellsford in North Auckland to Northern Waitakeres. Inhabits open country, bush margins and coast.

Characteristics: Large bird with heavy bill. Wary. Often seen perched on posts or power poles.

Voice: Loud 'koo-koo-koo-kooah-ha-ha'. Usually heard in early morning and sometimes when birds are flying.

Food: Insects and their larvae, lizards, mice and small birds.

Breeding: Tunnels are bored in rotten tree trunks. Also use cavities in coastal pohutukawas. Clutch of 2–4 white eggs is laid from November to February. Incubation 23 days. Chicks often do not survive, probably due to food shortage.

Opposite: New Zealand Kingfisher, male, at its nest hole in rotten tree.
Kookaburra.

Order PASSERIFORMES: Perching birds
Family ACANTHISITTIDAE: New Zealand Wrens
Genus *Acanthisitta*

South Island Rifleman *Acanthisitta chloris chloris* (Titipounamu). 8 cm.

North Island Rifleman *Acanthisitta chloris granti.* 8 cm.

Habitat and distribution: Apart from presence on Little and Great Barrier Islands, the North Island Rifleman inhabits native and exotic forests south of Te Aroha. South Island Rifleman inhabits exotic and native forests throughout South Island, especially in high-altitude beech forests.

Characteristics: Rifleman is New Zealand's smallest bird. Recognised by short tail and brisk movements, often spiralling around tree trunks when feeding.

Voice: A very high-pitched 'zit-zit'.

Food: Insects and their larvae and spiders.

Breeding: Nest is a globe of fine grasses and moss, lined with feathers, built under flaking bark, knot-hole in tree or in bank. Clutch of 3 or 4 white eggs is laid from September to January. Both sexes incubate for 20 days. Chicks are often fed by immature birds of previous nestings.

South Island Rifleman.

Above left: South Island Rifleman.
Above right: North Island Rifleman.
South Island Rifleman near nest hole.

Genus *Xenicus*

Rock Wren *Xenicus gilviventris.* 9 cm.

Habitat and distribution: Found only in South Island. Inhabits alpine and subalpine fell-fields and in scrub growing over tumbled rocks.

Characteristics: Slightly larger than Rifleman, with long legs and large feet. Habit of bobbing up and down. A weak flier. Lives under snow in rock crevices during winter.

Voice: An occasional high-pitched 'zit'.

Food: Insects and spiders.

Breeding: Nests from October to January. Globe-shaped nest of grasses lined with feathers built in rock crevices or fissures. Two or three white eggs are incubated by both sexes for 20 days.

Male Rock Wren.

Rock Wren, male.
Rock Wren, female.

Family ALAUDIDAE
Genus *Alauda*

Skylark *Alauda arvensis.* 18 cm.

Habitat and distribution: Introduced from Europe in 1860s. Inhabit open country, farmland, sand dunes and subalpine herb fields. Common throughout New Zealand.

Characteristics: Plumper build and less confiding than Pipit. Head crest.

Voice: Soars high, singing a continuous trilling song.

Food: Insects, their larvae, spiders and seeds.

Breeding: Nest of a few fine grasses is built in depression in ground, usually in short pasture. Three to five greyish, heavily speckled eggs are laid from September to January. Incubation, only by female, for 11 days. Both parents feed chicks.

Skylark at nest.
Below: Skylark in sand dune habitat.

Family MOTACILLIDAE
Genus *Anthus*

New Zealand Pipit *Anthus novaeseelandiae novaeseelandiae* (Pihoihoi). 19 cm.

Habitat and distribution: Inhabits rough grasslands, sand dunes and rocky terrain throughout New Zealand. Often lives at high altitudes.

Characteristics: Persistent tail flicking. Slimmer than Skylark. Does not soar high.

Voice: Slightly rasping 'zuit' or 'cheet'.

Food: Insects and their larvae, sandhoppers, kelp flies, also seeds.

Breeding: Nest of grasses is built in rough grass and herbage, often under a plant, usually on side of bank. Clutch of 3 or 4 cream-coloured eggs with dark blotches is laid September to February. Double brooded. Incubation by female for 15 days. Both parents feed chicks.

New Zealand Pipit.
Below: New Zealand Pipit at nest.

Family HIRUNDINIDAE: Swallows
Genus *Hirundo*

Welcome Swallow *Hirundo tahitica neoxena.* 15 cm.

Habitat and distribution: A recent colonist, arriving in Northland from Australia in the 1950s. The Welcome Swallow is now common throughout New Zealand near lakes, rivers, swamps and seashore.

Characteristics: Swift circling flight, sometimes splashing on surface of water. Often seen in groups perched on fences or telephone lines.

Voice: A high-pitched 'zwitt', also a chatter.

Food: Insects caught on wing. In winter often feeds on kelp flies on beaches.

Breeding: Builds nest of mud and grasses lined with feathers, attached to wall of culvert, bridge or ledges of buildings. Three or more broods a year from August to February. Lays clutch of 3–5 pale-pink eggs spotted with brown. Incubation by female for 15 days. Both parents feed chicks, which fledge when 18 days old.

Welcome Swallow.

Welcome Swallows.
Welcome Swallow flying to nest.

Family MUSCICAPIDAE: Warblers, Flycatchers, Thrushes. Genus *Turdus*

Blackbird *Turdus merula.* 25 cm.

Habitat and distribution: Introduced from Europe in 1860s. Common throughout New Zealand in gardens, parks, orchards and farmlands. Also found in depths of native forest, where it is extremely wary.

Characteristics: Male black with orange bill. Female brown.

Voice: Melodious flute-like whistle. Alarm note is a cackle.

Food: Insects, grubs and earthworms. Wide variety of fruits, including native podocarps, shrubs and nikau palm. Cause damage in orchards.

Breeding: Three or more broods a year. Bulky nest of twigs, leaves and grasses fortified with mud holds 3–5 greenish-coloured eggs blotched with light brown, laid from July to January. Female incubates for 13 days. Both parents feed chicks. Fledge 14 days.

Male Blackbird sunning.

Male Blackbird.
Female Blackbird at nest.

Genus *Turdus*

Song Thrush *Turdus philomelos.* 23 cm.

Habitat and distribution: Introduced from Europe in 1860s. Common throughout New Zealand in gardens, parks, orchards and farmlands. Also high country above 1500 metres. Rarely seen in depths of forest.

Characteristics: Sexes similar. When feeding, hops and runs, then remains motionless.

Voice: Harsher than blackbird song. Passages repeated three times and followed by pause and descending notes.

Food: Insects, grubs and earthworms, also snails broken open on favourite rock. Also takes some fruits.

Breeding: Several broods from June to January. Nest of twigs and grasses with lining of mud built in shrubs. Lays 3–5 blue eggs with black spots. Incubation by female for 12 days. Both parents feed chicks, which fledge at 14 days.

Song Thrush.
Below: Song Thrush at nest.

Family PRUNELLIDAE
Genus *Prunella*

Hedge Sparrow (Dunnock) *Prunella modularis.* 14 cm.

Habitat and distribution: Introduced from Europe in 1860s. Inhabits open country with shrubs and scrub. Seen in fell-fields at over 1000 metres and in suburban gardens throughout New Zealand.

Characteristics: Secretive, usually staying close to cover. Often heard singing in gardens, yet unseen.

Voice: A melodious, high-pitched warbled whistle.

Food: Insects, spiders, grubs and small earthworms, also a few seeds.

Breeding: A very neat nest composed of fine grasses and moss is built in thick shrub. Three or four bright turquoise-coloured eggs are laid from September to January. Double brooded. Incubation by hen for 11 days. Both parents feed chicks. Fledge 12 days.

Hedge Sparrow.

Family SYLVIIDAE
Genus *Bowdleria*

North Island Fernbird *Bowdleria punctata vealeae* (Matata). 18 cm.
South Island Fernbird *Bowdleria punctata punctata*. 18 cm.

Habitat and distribution: North Island Fernbird is common in swamps of Northland and central Volcanic Plateau, also in flax and scrub, uncommon in southern regions. South Island subspecies has a restricted range and is uncommon in Canterbury.

Characteristics: Sparrow-sized; tail with disjointed barbs. A very weak flier and rarely seen unless flushed. Responds well to tape-recorded calls. Mouse-like progression through undergrowth. The South Island Fernbird has larger dark spots on breast. The **Stewart Island Fernbird** *B.p. stewartiana* has more golden plumage.

Voice: At least five different calls. Common 'u-tick' uttered by two birds as contact. Male calls 'too-lit' with rising second note, also single 'trup'.

Food: Entirely insects, grubs and nursery-web spiders.

Breeding: Loose cup of dried grasses, lined with few feathers, is built in sedges or raupo, usually 15 cm above ground or water, but sometimes over 1 metre in matted *plagianthus*. The clutch of 2–4 pinkish-coloured eggs with brown spots is laid from September to January. Both sexes incubate for 14 or 15 days.

North Island Fernbird, typical habitat.

North Island Fernbird at nest.
North Island Fernbird.

Family PACHYCEPHALIDAE
Genus *Mohoua*

Whitehead *Mohoua albicilla* (Popokatea). 15 cm.

Habitat and distribution: Inhabits forest and scrub in the North Island. Apart from good populations on Little Barrier Island and Tiritiri Island, does not occur north of Te Aroha.

Characteristics: After nesting season, Whiteheads move noisily around canopy of forest in small groups. Readily respond to squeaker.

Voice: Repeated 'chip' or 'zwit' as birds move around in groups. Male's song is a soft, canary-like trill and whistle.

Food: Insects and grubs from foliage and bark. Often hang upside down. Also take fruits and seed.

Breeding: Often polygamous, with 3 or 4 birds attending a nest and feeding chicks. The nest, composed of grasses, moss and lichen, is often lined with tree-fern scales and a few feathers. Built in shrub or fork of tree. Clutch of 3 or 4 pinkish-coloured eggs is laid from October to January. Incubated by both sexes, or often 2 females, for 17 days.

Whitehead on nest in mingimingi shrub.

Whitehead.
Below: Whitehead and nest.

Genus *Mohoua*

Yellowhead *Mohoua achrocephala* (Mohua). 15 cm.

Habitat and distribution: Reasonable populations now only in Fiordland and Arthur's Pass National Park in South Island.

Characteristics: Usually seen in groups feeding in canopy. As it is confined to forest, mainly beech, the Yellowhead is not easily confused with introduced Yellowhammer of the open country.

Voice: Loud trill and rattling call.

Food: Feed mainly in canopy on insects, their larvae and spiders. Also take fruits.

Breeding: Build nest similar to that of Whitehead but site it in a hole or cavity in tree. Often polygamous, and male does not appear to assist in incubating the 2–4 pinkish eggs with brown spots. Incubation period 20 or 21 days.

Yellowhead at nest hole.

Genus *Mohoua*

Brown Creeper *Mohoua novaeseelandiae* (Pipipi). 13 cm.

Habitat and distribution: Inhabits native and exotic forests and scrub. Widespread and common in South Island only.

Characteristics: Seen in small flocks after nesting season. A small, brown, active and inquisitive bird.

Voice: A rapid 'chi-chi-tee-tee'.

Food: Insects and their larvae and spiders, also small fruits.

Breeding: Builds nest of leaves, mosses and lichens bound with cobweb, sited in dense shrub or manuka. Favourite site is in lawyer vine growing over matagouri. Clutch of 2–4 cream-coloured eggs with dark-brown markings are laid from September to February. Incubation by female for 17 days. Both parents feed chicks.

Brown Creeper.

Family ACANTHIZIDAE: Australian warblers
Genus *Gerygone*

Grey Warbler *Gerygone igata* (Riroriro). 11 cm.

Habitat and distribution: Common throughout New Zealand in native and exotic forests and scrub. Usually seen in pairs or small family groups.

Characteristics: Small size, overall grey colour and continuous activity distinguish it from other species. Easily attracted to squeaker.

Voice: A melodious, wavering warble with song ended abruptly. Alarm note a repeated twitter.

Food: Feeds entirely on insects, their larvae and spiders.

Breeding: Three broods a year, commencing in August. Second brood in October often parasiticised by Shining Cuckoo. Hanging nest built of moss, lichens, strips of bark and grasses, with dome and entrance at one side, and liberally lined with feathers. Clutch of 3 or 4 pink eggs with brown spots is incubated by female for 18 days.

Opposite: Grey Warbler at nest.
Grey Warbler and nest in kahikatea.

Family MONARCHIDAE
Genus *Rhipidura*

North Island Fantail *Rhipidura fuliginosa placabilis* (Piwakawaka).
16 cm.
South Island Fantail *Rhipidura fuliginosa fuliginosa*. 16 cm.

Habitat and distribution: Common in forests, scrub, suburban
gardens and exotic pine forests throughout New Zealand.

Characteristics: Black form of Fantail more common in South
Island. North Island Fantail has half of each outer tail feather white;
three-quarters of these feathers are white in South Island Fantail.

Voice: Single sharp 'cheet' is contact call. Male has chattering song
of several syllables.

Food: Entirely insectivorous. Most insects caught on the wing. The
fanned tail may act as sweep to disturb insects. Often flocks feed on
grass paddocks in winter, sometimes landing on ground.

Breeding: Nest from August to February, with 4 or 5 broods a year.
Clutch of 2 or 3 pale cream-coloured eggs with brown spots
incubated by both sexes for 15 days.

North Island Fantail.

Above left: Fantail chicks close to fledging.
Above right: Typical Fantail nest with 'tail'.
Fantail nest in tanekaha.

Family EOPSALTRIIDAE
Genus *Petroica*

North Island Tomtit *Petroica macrocephala toitoi* (Miromiro). 13 cm.
South Island Tomtit *Petroica macrocephala macrocephala* (Ngiru-ngiru). 13 cm.

Habitat and distribution: Inhabit forested areas and tall scrub throughout New Zealand.

Characteristics: Some South Island Tomtit males have yellow or orange breasts while others have white breasts, as in North Island subspecies. Males are inquisitive and more often seen than the brownish-coloured females.

Voice: Contact call is high-pitched 'tee-tee'. Male sings with a warbling 'yodi-yodi-yodi'.

Food: Insects, their larvae, spiders and earthworms.

Breeding: Nests of lichens, bark, moss and grasses bound with cobwebs are built in tree cavities, ends of broken branches, under banks or in dead fronds on trunk of tree fern. Clutch of 3–5 cream-coloured eggs with brown markings is laid from August to January and incubated by female for 17 days. Both parents feed chicks, and after first brood is part grown, female builds second nest while male attends chicks.

Left: Male South Island Tomtit.
Right: Immature female South Island Tomtit.

Male North Island Tomtit at nest.
Female North Island Tomtit at nest.

Genus *Petroica*

North Island Robin *Petroica australis longipes* (Toutouwai). 18 cm.
South Island Robin *Petroica australis australis*. 18 cm.
Stewart Island Robin *Petroica australis rakiura*. 18 cm.

Habitat and distribution: Widely distributed in native and exotic forests and manuka scrub. Absent north of Te Aroha except for Little Barrier Island.

Characteristics: Robins are confiding and approach humans to feed in areas of litter disturbed by feet.

Voice: Song is a plaintive 'tweep-tweep' leading to a slow warble. Sometimes sing without pause for up to an hour.

Food: Insects, including large prey such as stick insects and wetas, grubs, spiders and earthworms.

Breeding: Bulky nest composed of leaves, small sticks, grasses and moss, is built in tree fork, hollow of tree or end of broken limb. Clutch of 3 or 4 cream-coloured eggs with dark-brown spots is laid from October to January. Double brooded. Female incubates for 18–20 days. Both sexes feed chicks.

North Island Robin at nest.

North Island Robin.
South Island Robin.

Family ZOSTEROPIDAE
Genus *Zosterops*

Silvereye *Zosterops lateralis lateralis* (Tauhou). 12 cm.

Habitat and distribution: Widespread and common in native and exotic forests, scrub, orchards and suburban gardens.

Characteristics: Self-introduced to New Zealand from Australia in 1856. Usually seen in small groups moving rapidly through foliage. Visits garden bird-tables for bread, fruit and sugar-water.

Voice: Contact call is sharp 'twee'. Male sings with subdued warbling trills.

Food: Insects, grubs, spiders, small fruits and nectar. Silvereyes also cause damage to orchard fruits.

Breeding: Clutch of 2 or 3 pale-blue eggs is laid in a flimsy, ladle-like nest composed of fine grasses, hairs, moss and spider web. This is suspended from twigs of shrubs or bamboo. Incubation by both sexes for 12 days.

Silvereye.

Silvereyes.
Silvereye and nest.

Family MELIPHAGIDAE
Genus *Notiomystis*

Stitchbird *Notiomystis cincta* (Hihi). 19 cm.

Habitat and distribution: Common in forests of Little Barrier Island. Recently introduced to Hen and Kapiti Islands.

Characteristics: Male easily recognised as unlike any other species. Female somewhat resembles female Bellbird.

Voice: A high-pitched, penetrating 't-zee'. Male has subdued, warbling song.

Food: Nectar from variety of flowers, also fruits, insects and grubs.

Breeding: Nest of small rootlets, sticks and fine grasses built in hole in tree. Clutch of 3 or 4 white eggs is laid from October to January and incubated by female for approximately 17 days. Both sexes feed chicks.

Stitchbird, male.

Stitchbird, female.
Stitchbird, immature female.

Genus *Anthornis*

Bellbird *Anthornis melanura melanura* (Makomako). 20 cm.

Habitat and distribution: Common in native and exotic forests, orchards and gardens. Apart from stray male Bellbirds from offshore islands, the species is not found in Auckland or Northland. Different subspecies of Bellbird inhabit Three Kings and Poor Knights Islands.

Characteristics: Recognised by slight downcurve of bill and shallow fork in tail.

Voice: Surprisingly loud voice in relation to size. Dawn song consists of 3–5 bell-like notes. Daytime song resembles that of Tui but notes are more pure and contain fewer guttural sounds.

Food: Nectar, fruits, insects and spiders. Males take far more nectar than females. Latter take more insects.

Breeding: Two broods a year are raised between September and January. Nest of twigs, leaves and grasses built in shrub, fork of tree or in shallow tree cavity. Female incubates the 3- or 4-egg clutch of pinkish eggs with brown spots for 13 or 14 days.

Bellbird, male.

Female Bellbird at nest.
Male Bellbird singing.

Genus *Prosthemadera*

Tui *Prosthemadera novaeseelandiae novaeseelandiae.* 30 cm.

Habitat and distribution: Inhabit forests and forest remnants, orchards and gardens throughout New Zealand.

Characteristics: Conspicuous white throat feathers. Strong, rapid, noisy flight. Males larger than females and immature birds.

Voice: Song varies considerably with district. Bell-like notes, low whistles, chuckles and guttural 'squarks' are all part of repertoire.

Food: Nectar, fruits and insects. Often takes large insects such as stick insects. Fly considerable distances to feed on seasonal flowering plants, e.g. kowhai and pohutukawa.

Breeding: A bulky nest of sticks, dry leaves and grasses is built in tree fork, shrub or manuka canopy. Clutch of 2 or 3 pinkish eggs with light-brown spots is laid from September to January and incubated by female for 14 days. Both parents feed chicks.

Tui.

Above left: Tuis at nest.
Above right: Tui singing.
Tui, female.

Family EMBERIZIDAE
Genus *Emberiza*

Cirl Bunting *Emberiza cirlus*. 16 cm.

Habitat and distribution: Introduced from Britain in 1870s. Inhabits open country with scrub in drier areas of Marlborough, Nelson and North Canterbury. Very uncommon elsewhere.

Characteristics: Greyish-brown rump distinguishes it from Yellowhammer, which has russet-coloured rump. Male has black bib.

Voice: A contact 'zitt' note. Song is a high-pitched, buzzing rattle.

Food: Mainly seeds, but also insects.

Breeding: Nest of dried grasses built low down in thick shrub. Clutch of 2–4 greenish-grey eggs with dark streaks is incubated by female for 13 days.

Left: Cirl Bunting, male.
Right: Cirl Bunting, female.

Genus *Emberiza*

Yellowhammer *Emberiza citrinella.* 16 cm.

Habitat and distribution: Introduced from Europe in 1860s. Very common in open country, scrub and sand dunes. Very large flocks congregate in winter to feed on paddocks.

Characteristics: Male Yellowhammer yellower than female. Latter resembles female Cirl Bunting apart from russet-coloured rump.

Voice: Contact note is a metallic 'tink'. Males have song of 9 or 10 notes.

Food: Mainly seeds from grasses and many other plants. Also takes insects, grubs and spiders.

Breeding: Nest of dry grasses and moss built low down in thick herbage, especially in brambles. Clutch of 3 or 4 pinkish eggs with 'pencil marks' and dark spots. Incubation by female for 13 days.

Left: Male Yellowhammer singing.
Right: Female Yellowhammer.

Family FRINGILLIDAE
Genus *Fringilla*

Chaffinch *Fringilla coelabs.* 15 cm.

Habitat and distribution: Our commonest finch. Introduced from Europe in 1860s, it inhabits open country with trees, suburban parks and gardens, and is often found in the depths of native and exotic forests.

Characteristics: Usually call note is heard in forest before bird is seen. Often feeds on ground.

Voice: Common call note is a metallic 'chink'. Male's song is a bright 'chip-chip-chip-pell-pell-cheery-cheery-cheeoo'.

Food: Mainly seeds, which are crushed, not opened as with other finches. Also fruits and insects.

Breeding: An extremely neat, well camouflaged nest of grasses and lichens is built in a tree fork or shrub. Clutch of 3–5 greyish-coloured eggs with purple spots is laid from September to January and incubated by female for 12 days.

Chaffinch, male.

Chaffinch, female.
Chaffinch, male at nest.

Genus *Carduelis*

Greenfinch *Carduelis chloris.* 15 cm.

Habitat and distribution: Introduced from Europe in 1860s. Inhabit open country, orchards and suburban gardens.

Characteristics: Common throughout New Zealand. Form large flocks during autumn and winter.

Voice: A buzzing 'zwee'.

Food: Mainly seeds from grasses and other plants, also insects.

Breeding: Largish nest of twigs, grasses and moss is built in fork of shrubs. Clutch of 3 or 4 light-grey eggs with brown spots and blotches is laid from September to January. Incubated by female for 11 or 12 days.

Male Greenfinch feeding female.

Genus *Carduelis*

Goldfinch *Carduelis carduelis*. 12.5 cm.

Habitat and distribution: Introduced from Britain in 1860s and now commoner here than in country of origin. Inhabits orchards, open country with trees and suburban gardens.

Characteristics: Small size and bright plumage distinguish it from other finches. Forms very large flocks of over 1000 birds in open country in winter.

Voice: A high-pitched 'piew'.

Food: Variety of seeds. Often feeds on seeds from Scotch thistles.

Breeding: Neat nest of grasses, moss and lichens, lined with thistledown, is often built in orchard trees or gorse. Clutch of 3–6 light-grey eggs with dark spots is incubated by female for 11 days. Male feeds her on nest.

Goldfinch.

Genus *Carduelis*

Redpoll *Carduelis flammea*. 12 cm.

Habitat and distribution: Redpolls inhabit open country. Often seen at high altitudes, they also live in scrub and sand dunes throughout New Zealand.

Characteristics: Introduced from Europe in 1860s, this is the smallest finch. Has undulating flight. Pink breast of male is seen at close quarters.

Voice: A constant twitter in flight.

Food: Seeds and shoots. Also eat buds of fruit trees in orchards.

Breeding: Compact nest of grasses and moss, lined with wool or hair, is built in low bushes, especially gorse. Clutch of 3–5 greenish eggs with dark-brown spots is incubated by females for 11 days.

Redpoll.

PHOTO D.W. HADDEN

Family PLOCEIDAE
Genus *Passer*

House Sparrow *Passer domesticus.* 14 cm.

Habitat and distribution: Very common throughout New Zealand in farmland, parks and suburban gardens.

Characteristics: Introduced to New Zealand in 1860s. Gregarious and usually seen in small flocks. Roost in flocks. Male has black bib.

Voice: Chirps and chatters.

Food: Wide variety of seeds, green foliage of vegetables, fruits of native plants and trees. Causes damage to cereal crops.

Breeding: Bulky, untidy domed nest composed of grasses and lined with feathers, is built in trees, cavities of cliffs and in buildings. The clutch of 3–6 eggs of very variable colours, mainly grey and spotted, is incubated by both sexes.

House Sparrow, male at left, with two females.

Family STURNIDAE
Genus *Sturnus*

Starling *Sturnus vulgaris*. 21 cm.

Habitat and distribution: Introduced from Europe in 1860s. Starlings inhabit open country, farm pastures, parks, suburban gardens and seashores. They feed and roost in large flocks. Common thoughout New Zealand.

Characteristics: After summer moult birds have spotted plumage. Tips of feathers later wear to produce spring glossy plumage.

Voice: Guttural warblings and chuckles. Accurately imitate other birds' calls.

Food: Wide range of insects, grubs, earthworms, snails, small fruits and nectar from flax flowers. Also takes fruit from native trees such as kahikatea.

Breeding: Nests, often extremely bulky, are composed of grasses, small sticks, paper, leaves and feathers, and built in tree holes, crevices in cliffs and in buildings. Starlings readily use garden nestboxes. Clutch of 3–5 pale-blue eggs is laid in October or November. Both parents incubate for 11 days. Chicks fledge when 18 days old.

Starling.

238

Above left: Starling in autumn plumage.
Above right: Starling in early summer plumage.
Newly fledged Starling chicks.

Genus *Acridotheres*

Common Myna *Acridotheres tristis*. 24 cm.

Habitat and distribution: Introduced from India in 1870s, the Myna inhabits open country, suburban areas and rubbish tips throughout North Island. Very common in Northland but absent from South Island.

Characteristics: Seen in small groups after nesting season. Use communal roosts in thick shrubs or bamboo.

Voice: Raucous squawking, chattering and gurgling.

Food: Insects, grubs, earthworms, fruits and carrion. Mynas also predate nests of small birds and evict starlings from nests.

Breeding: Bulky nest, composed of small sticks, grasses, leaves, paper, plastic and feathers, is built in hole in tree, rock crevice, building or disused kingfisher burrows. Mynas are late nesters, laying 2 or 3 pale-blue eggs from late November to January. Incubation, mainly by female, for 14 days.

Common Myna.

Common Myna flying to nest.
Common Myna at nest hole.

Family CALLAEIDAE
Genus *Callaeas*

North Island Kokako *Callaeas cinerea wilsoni.* 38 cm.

Habitat and distribution: Inhabit unmodified lowland forests of central North Island, North Taranaki, mixed kauri forests in Northland, (Puketi Forest). Some still survive in Coromandel forests and on Great Barrier Island. (South Island Kokako probably extinct.)

Characteristics: A weak flier, the Kokako progresses through forest with bounds and glides. Skulking in habit. Best viewed soon after dawn, when birds sing from prominent perch.

Voice: Melodious flute-like notes with mews and clucks; some passages are reminiscent of Tui.

Food: Mainly vegetarian. Eats wide range of foliage, flowers and fruits; also takes small insects, especially when nesting.

Breeding: Bulky nest with base of sticks covered with thick bed of moss is built in dense supplejack vine or shrub. Clutch of 2 or 3 cream-coloured eggs with brown spots is laid from November to March and incubated by hen for 20 days. Both parents feed chicks at approximately 20-minute intervals. They raise a second brood in season if sufficient food is available. Chicks fledge when $4^1/_2$ weeks old and accompany parent for several weeks.

North Island Kokako.

Above left: North Island Kokako,
showing small rounded wings.
Centre: North Island Kokako, pair
at nest.
Above right: North Island Kokako.
Below: North Island Kokako at
nest.

243

Genus *Philesturnus*

North Island Saddleback *Philesturnus carunculatus rufusater* (Tieke).
25 cm.
South Island Saddleback *Philesturnus carunculatus carunculatus*.
25 cm.

Habitat and distribution: North Island Saddleback inhabits several offshore islands on east coast of North Island and Kapiti Island, following transfers from Hen Island in 1964. South Island subspecies inhabits islands off coast of Stewart Island.

Characteristics: North Island Saddleback has narrow, buff-coloured band in front of saddle. Immature South Island Saddleback lacks a saddle and is uniform olive-brown colour. Saddlebacks are weak fliers, but are very active, with rapid movements through forest.

Voice: Usual call is penetrating 'cheep-tee-tee-tee'. Male has several more melodious calls.

Food: Mainly insects, grubs, spiders and other invertebrates caught from foliage and prised from under bark. Also takes fruits.

Breeding: Nest, built in hollow in tree or rock crevice, is constructed of small sticks and grasses. Clutch of 2 buff eggs with brown spots is laid from November to January and incubated for 20 days by the hen, who is fed at nest by male. Both sexes feed chicks, which fledge when 21 days old. Two broods in season.

Left: North Island Saddleback, male.
Right: North Island Saddleback, immature.

244

North Island Saddleback, male.
North Island Saddleback, female at nest hole.

Family CRACTICIDAE
Genus *Gymnorhina*

Australian Magpie *Gymnorhina tibicen*. 42 cm.

Habitat and distribution: Introduced from Australia in 1860s, this Magpie is now widespread in open country throughout New Zealand, especially farm pastures with trees.

Characteristics: Two subspecies: White-backed Magpie *G.t.hypoleuca* and Black-backed Magpie *G.t.tibicen*. Frequently interbreed. White-backed and Black-backed females and juveniles have grey-flecked backs.

Voice: A melodious warble of flute-like notes.

Food: Omnivorous. Wide variety of invertebrates, seeds, vegetation and carrion. Also lizards and eggs and young from ground-nesting birds.

Breeding: In the north often nests as early as June. Nest of sticks lined with grasses and wool is built in fork of tree, especially pines and macrocarpa. Clutch of 2–4 grey-blue eggs with dark blotches is incubated by female for 20 days. Both sexes feed chicks.

Left: White-backed Magpie, female.
Right: White-backed Magpie, male at nest.

Family CORVIDAE
Genus *Corvus*

Rook *Corvus frugilegus*. 45 cm.

Habitat and distribution: Introduced from Europe in.1870s.
Widely distributed in farmlands from Northern Hawke's Bay to
Wairarapa, with smaller populations in Canterbury and Miranda,
Firth of Thames.

Characteristics: A wary bird. Usually seen in groups feeding on
farmland. Roosts at night in communal roosts.

Voice: Repeated 'kaaw'.

Food: Wide range of invertebrates, foliage of plants and walnuts.
Frequently damage growing vegetable crops.

Breeding: Nest in colonies called rookeries, in pines, gums and oak
trees. Built of sticks and lined with grasses and wool, the nest is
sometimes reinforced with mud. Clutch of 3–6 greenish-coloured
eggs with dark brown blotches is incubated by female for 17 or 18
days. Fed on nest by male. Chicks fledge when 33 days old.

Rook at nest.

Bibliography

The Atlas of Bird Distribution in New Zealand, by the Ornithological Society of New Zealand Inc., eds. P. C. Bull, P. C. Gaze., and C. J. R. Robertson. (1985).

The Birds Around Us, by Geoff Moon. (Heinemann, 1979).

Birds of the Water, Wood and Waste, by H. Guthrie Smith. (Whitcombe and Tombs Ltd, 1927).

Checklist of the Birds of New Zealand, by the Checklist Committee (E. G. Turbott, Convener), Ornithological Society of New Zealand, Inc. (Random Century, 1990).

Collins Guide to the Birds of New Zealand, by R. A. Falla, R. B. Sibson and E. G. Turbott. (Collins, 1986).

Eric Hosking's Waders, text by W. G. Hale. (Pelham Books Ltd, 1983).

Field Guide to Australian Birds, by Peter Slater. (Rigby Ltd, 1970).

Handbook of British Birds, Vols 1–5, by H. F. Witherby, F. C. R. Jourdain, N. F. Ticehurst and B. W. Tucker. (H. F. & G. Witherby Ltd, 1944).

New Zealand Birds, by M. F. Soper. (Whitcombe and Tombs Ltd, 1972).

New Zealand's Birds, Geoff Moon and Ronald Lockley. (Heinemann, 1982).

New Zealand Nature Heritage (Part works), ed. C. A. Fleming. (Hamlyn, 1974).

Ocean Wanderers, by Ronald M. Lockley. (David and Charles, 1974).

Refocus on New Zealand Birds, by G. Moon. (A. H. & A. W. Reed, 1967).

Scientific American: Birds (W. H. Freeman & Co., 1980).

Seabirds, by Delphine Haley. (Pacific Search Press, 1984).

Seabirds, by Peter Harrison. (Croom Helm Ltd & A. H. & A. W. Reed, 1983).

Shorebirds, by Peter Hayman, John Marchant and Tony Prater. (Croom Helm, 1986).

Shorebirds of Australia, by John Douglas Pringle. (Angus and Robertson, 1987).

Southern Albatrosses and Petrels, by Peter C. Harper and F. C. Kinsky. (Price Milburn, 1978).

Trees and Shrubs of New Zealand, by A. L. Poole and N. M. Adams. (Government Printer, 1963).

Wading Birds of the World, by Eric and Richard Soothill. (Blandford Press, 1982).

Index of Common Names

Index of Scientific Names

252

Notes

Notes

Notes

Notes